TELL ME WHY #5

BY ARKADY LEOKUM

ILLUSTRATIONS BY KATHIE KELLEHER

COVER ILLUSTRATION BY PAUL VAN MUNCHING

GROSSET & DUNLAP • New York

CONTENTS

Chapter 1

How Things Began

When did horse racing begin? 7
Who invented the elevator? 8
When did the first fire department
    begin? 9
Where was the first theater? 10
Who were the first barbers? 10
Why are London policemen called
    "Bobbies"? 11
Who first made bread with yeast? 12
When did the sport of surfing begin? 13
How did the words in the English
    language originate? 14
How did we learn to write? 15
Who invented comic books? 15
What is the origin of the dog? 16
When were the first keys made? 17
Why do we have April Fools' Day? 18
Who set up the arrangement of
    typewriter keys? 19
When were gems discovered? 20
How were time zones decided? 20
When were cows first used for milk? 22
Where was rice first grown? 22
Why was the metric system
    invented? 23
Who invented traffic signals? 24
Why is speed at sea measured in
    knots? 24
When did people begin to pierce
    their ears? 25
Who were the first people to make
    mummies? 26

Why do we have Christmas trees? 27
Why was Washington D.C. made
    the capital of the United States? 28
How did the name "Uncle Sam"
    originate? 28
How old is the game of checkers? 29
When were the first museums
    opened? 30
Who invented the violin? 30
Who invented musical notes? 32
Why do soldiers salute? 32
When did athletics begin? 33
Who invented indoor plumbing? 34
When was jewelry first worn? 34

Chapter 2

Our World

How does water put out a fire? 36
How are amendments added to the
    Constitution? 37
How does the soil help plants grow? 37
How do seeds grow? 38
What are diatoms? 39
When did plants appear on earth? 40
Who carved the faces on Mount
    Rushmore? 41
When was the Great Sphinx built? 42
Are the continents moving? 43
What is magma? 43
Why is lava hot? 44
Why does the moon have different
    shapes? 45

Why is there no life on the moon? 46
Do other planets move like the earth? 47
What makes a beautiful sunset? 47
What is the difference between toadstools and mushrooms? 48
How was petroleum formed in the earth? 49
Why does a cactus have spines? 49
What is an earthquake belt? 51
Where does money for taxes go? 51
What is inflation? 52
Why don't all countries have a common form of money? 53
What is a stock? 53
What is ecology? 54
How were the Great Lakes formed? 55
What is olive oil? 56
What is the highest mountain in the world? 57
Why is it cooler on top of a mountain? 57
Why did Indians take scalps? 58
Has the Ice Age really ended? 58
What is a folk song? 59
Do any cannibals exist today? 60
Did the Vikings visit North America? 60
What are aborigines? 62
What is witchcraft? 62
Where do metals come from? 63
Who discovered atoms? 64
What is the ozone layer? 65

Chapter 3

The Human Body

What causes an earache? 66
What is yellow fever? 67
Why is there still no cure for cancer? 68
What is cerebral palsy? 69
How does the brain send messages to the body? 69
Why do we need oxygen? 71
What is endocrinology? 71
What is hemoglobin? 72
How do we swallow? 73
Why do we smoke? 74

What are phagocytes? 75
Why do we need so much sleep? 75
What changes the rate of a heartbeat? 76
Why do alcoholic beverages make you drunk? 77
What causes gout? 77
What gives food its taste? 78
How fast does our blood flow? 79
What vitamins do we need? 79
Why is hair different colors? 80
What makes hair curly? 81
Why do we get sunburned? 81
Where do warts come from? 83
How are bacteria useful to man? 83

Chapter 4

How Things Are Made

What causes cement to harden? 85
How can a diamond be cut? 86
What is a detergent? 87
How are colors formed? 88
What is a photoelectric cell? 88
What is music? 90
What is irrigation? 90
How is carbon-14 used to date objects? 91
What is an autopsy? 92
Why do golf balls have holes? 93
Are horses used to make glue? 94
How can the distance to a star be measured? 95
How are raisins made from grapes? 96
What is leather? 96
How do Eskimos build igloos? 97
How can a helicopter hover in space? 98
Why does silver tarnish? 98
How is butter made? 99
Why does swiss cheese have holes? 100
How do scientists determine ocean depths? 100
What is virgin wool? 102
What makes gasoline burn? 102
Why is there lead in gasoline? 103
What is a satellite? 103

What is a laser beam? 105
What keeps you up on a moving
    bicycle? 105
What is incense made of? 106
What is a dam? 107
Where do they get iron to make
    steel? 108
How are bricks made? 109
How are synthetic fibers made? 109
What is sonar? 110

Chapter 5

How Other Creatures Live

What are eels? 112
Do hyenas really laugh? 113
Can snakes hear? 114
How often do snakes shed their
    skins? 115
What makes a rattlesnake
    poisonous? 115
What is the rattle of a rattlesnake
    made of? 116
Why can't the ostrich fly? 117
What do hornets use to make their
    nests? 118
How do bees sting? 118
How do worms crawl? 119
How are fish able to smell things? 120
Do all fish lay eggs? 120
How do jellyfish reproduce? 121
How do fish reproduce? 122
Do fish ever sleep? 122
What is a vulture? 123
When did horses come to North
    America? 124
How do scientists know animals are
    color blind? 125
How do we know bats use radar? 126
Do polar bears hibernate? 127
Why do opossums carry their
    young? 127
Can a butterfly smell? 128
Why do a cat's eyes glow in the
    dark? 129
Why do cats have whiskers? 130

How did the hippopotamus get its
    name? 130
What is a mammal? 131
What is a sloth? 132
When did reptiles first appear? 132
How do turtles breathe underwater? 134
Where are blue whales found? 134
Can birds smell? 135
Why do woodpeckers peck on trees? 136
How do snails get their shells? 136
What is the difference between
    bacteria and viruses? 137
What are lice? 138
Why do people hunt walruses? 139
What is the 17-year locust? 139
Where do penguins lay their eggs? 141
Why are dolphins considered
    intelligent? 141
When did man first find out about
    dinosaurs? 142
What is an amoeba? 143

Chapter 6

Love, Families, and Babies

At what age do people fall in love? 144
Is a mother's love for her children
    the same as her love for her
    husband? 144
Is it possible to love a friend as
    much as a sweetheart? 146
Can people of different races fall in
    love? 146
Why do people sometimes fall out of
    love? 146
As married people get older do they
    love each other less? 147
Do the children in a family always
    love each other? 147
Can a child hate his father or
    mother? 148
Why do we sometimes feel that
    nobody loves us? 148
Does a parent have to like the
    person we fall in love with? 149
If we "love" a pet, like a dog or a
    horse, is that really love? 149

Are there some people who never
  fall in love? 150
What does it mean to "love your
  fellow man"? 150
Do animals fall in love? 150
What does the heart have to do with
  love? 151
Can people who love each other live
  together without getting
  married? 151
Why do people go on honeymoons? 152
What is puberty? 153
What is adolescence? 153
Why does it usually take nine
  months for a baby to be born? 154
In what part of a woman's body
  does the baby develop? 154
How does a baby breathe inside the
  mother's body? 155
What exactly happens in the process
  of giving birth to a baby? 156
When does a baby's heart begin to
  beat? 156
Why are there sometimes twins or
  triplets instead of one baby? 157

What is an embryo? 157
What is a fetus? 158
Is it true that a human embryo has a
  tail? 159
How big is the embryo at the end of
  one month? 159
When does the fetus begin to look
  like a human baby? 160
How does the mother know when
  the baby is about to be born? 160
Is a baby always born head first? 161
Why do new babies cry so much? 161
Do babies learn how to suck milk? 162
Why do children resemble their
  parents? 162
What color would a baby be if one
  parent was black and one was
  white? 163
Why are babies "burped" after
  feeding? 163
How often is a newborn baby fed? 163
How many hours does a newborn
  baby sleep? 164

Index 167

CHAPTER 1
HOW
THINGS BEGAN

WHEN DID HORSE RACING BEGIN?

Using horses for racing seems to be one of the oldest sports enjoyed by man. Races between horses were run in very ancient times. They were held in Egypt, Babylonia, and Syria. Homer described a Greek chariot race that took place about eight centuries before the birth of Christ.

But modern horse racing as we know it originated in England, and it had to do with the development in England of the thoroughbred horse. There were horse races in England as early as the 12th century, but it was in the late 17th and early 18th centuries that the breeding of horses for sport really began.

Eastern horses were brought to England from Arabia, Turkey, and Persia. Stallions from these countries were bred to English mares. Three of these stallions were very important. They were called the Darley Arabian, the Godolphin Arabian, and the Byerly Turk. The lineage of every modern registered thoroughbred traces back to all three in the male line!

During the 18th century horse racing became an important English sport. The Jockey Club was established in 1751. And in 1793 the first issue of the "General Stud Book," which lists the lineage of thoroughbreds, was issued.

Horse racing has long been known as the "sport of kings." This is because English royalty has owned and raced champion horses, and because royalty and wealthy people in other countries have been involved with the sport.

In the United States, horse races were held in the early 17th century, even before the development of the thoroughbred.

TRACTION SHEAVE

HOISTING ROPES

CAR

SAFETY ROPE

COUNTER WEIGHT

OTIS ELECTRIC ELEVATOR

TRACTION ELEVATOR

WHO INVENTED THE ELEVATOR?

The idea of the elevator was invented by no one man; it was developed over a long period of time. This is because the mechanical principles of elevators had been in use for centuries.

The ancient Greeks knew how to lift objects, using pulleys and winches. A pulley is a grooved wheel that a rope can slide over. A winch is a machine that has a broad wheel, or drum, with a rope fastened to it. By turning the drum with a crank, the rope can be wound up on the drum or let out. By running the rope over a pulley, it can be made to raise or lower a load.

In the 17th century, a "flying chair" was invented. It was designed to carry people to the top floors of buildings and was operated by a system of weights and pulleys. The chair and its machinery were outside the building. The "flying chair" never became popular.

During the first half of the 19th century, elevators were already in existence, but they were mostly used for freight. Steam power was used to turn the hoisting drums of these elevators.

What people were afraid of was that the rope holding the elevator might snap and the elevator would go crashing down. Then Elisha Otis invented a safety device that prevented this from happening, and elevators became popular. Also, at this time hydraulic power (fluid under pressure) began to be used to raise and lower elevators.

The electric elevator, which is what is used today, was developed by the German engineer, Werner von Siemens.

WHEN DID THE FIRST FIRE DEPARTMENT BEGIN?

Long ago there were no regular firemen. If a house caught fire, everybody became a fire fighter. People formed bucket brigades to fight fires. They stood in line to make a human chain from the burning house to the river or well. They passed buckets of water along from hand to hand for those up front to pour on the flames.

In 1666 London had a fire that burned down 13,000 buildings, including St. Paul's Cathedral. The English then began to develop hand-operated pumps so fire fighters could spray water through a hose. Citizens began to join together in volunteer fire companies. These volunteers promised to drop everything and rush to fight fire whenever it broke out.

The first paid fire department was established in Boston in 1679. There had been a series of big fires there in 1653 and 1676. Boston ordered a hand-operated fire engine from England and appointed 13 men to man it.

The first volunteer fire department in the United States was founded in 1736 in Philadelphia by Benjamin Franklin. It replaced the bucket brigades that had existed up to then.

In 1835, New York City established its first paid fire patrol. There were four members who were paid $250 a year. The following year there were 40 members, who were known as Fire Police. The first firehouse was organized in 1855 in New York City.

Today, in the United States, there are about one thousand fire departments manned by fully paid professional firemen, and more than fifteen thousand other departments that are part-paid and volunteer. There are more than eighty thousand professional firemen in the United States and over eight hundred thousand volunteer firemen.

WHERE WAS THE FIRST THEATER?

Theater as we know it first developed in Greece as part of religious observance. The stage was simply a circle of turf on which the worshipers danced around the altar of Dionysus. The spot was usually at the foot of a hill so that the spectators on the slopes could watch the dancing.

This started the tradition of Greek theaters—semicircles of seats built into a hillside. In fact, the word "theater" is of Greek origin and means "a place for seeing."

A theater built in Athens about 500 B.C. had a circular place, called the orchestra, where the performance was given. Erected behind the circle of the orchestra was a dignified-looking stage building. It was used as a dressing place for the performers. This "skene" (from which comes the word "scene") served as a background for the action of the play. Very little scenery was used by the Greeks, and no artificial lighting was needed, because the plays were presented in the daytime.

The first permanent stone theater was built in Rome in 52 B.C. The theaters of the Romans were similar to those of the Greeks, except that they were built on level ground. The Romans were the first to fill the orchestra with seats and present the play on a raised stage behind which was the "skene."

After the Roman world turned Christian, no theaters were built for about a thousand years. The first modern theater was the Teatro Farnese at Parma, Italy. It was built in 1618 or 1619. Its stage, instead of projecting far out into the orchestra, was built into one of the walls. A curtain was used to separate the stage from the auditorium, so that changes of scenery could be made out of sight of the audience.

WHO WERE THE FIRST BARBERS?

There have been barbers since very ancient times—so long ago, in fact, that we can't possibly know who the first barbers were. The first records of barbers in history go back to ancient Egypt. Later on, in ancient Greece and Rome, barbershops were favorite meeting places where men discussed affairs of the day.

Everybody knows what the barber's pole looks like. Those red-and-white stripes have something to do with work that barbers did in olden days. In ancient times, doctors didn't want to have anything to do with surgery. So it was the barbers who performed surgery on patients. They did bloodletting (letting a patient bleed so that the "bad blood" or "sick blood" would leave the body). They treated wounds, and some of them even extracted teeth.

The barber's pole of red-and-white stripes goes back to those days. The red stands for blood, and the white for bandages.

In England the barbers were chartered as a guild as far back as 1462. In 1540, their guild was merged with the guild of surgeons. But about this time, the king of England forbade the barbers who cut hair and gave shaves to practice surgery.

In the next two hundred years, the work of the barber was separated more and more from that of the surgeon, and in time all they were allowed to do was give haircuts.

By the way, the word "barber" comes from the Latin word "barba," which meant "beard." So their work of trimming beards may have been more important than cutting hair.

WHY ARE LONDON POLICEMEN CALLED "BOBBIES"?

The idea of a police system to protect a city originated in London. In 1737 a law was passed creating a police system with 68 men. But as the city grew and poverty increased, looting and rioting were soon out of control in London.

In 1829 Sir Robert Peel formed the London Metropolitan Police, with headquarters in Scotland Yard. The new recruits wore top hats and tailcoats. But this new force that Peel had created was much larger, better trained, and more highly disciplined than any other police force had ever been.

The rioting in London was soon controlled, but before long it spread to other areas. As a result, in 1835 all towns and cities in England were empowered to form their own police departments. From Sir Robert Peel's name came the familiar nickname "bobby" for the English policeman.

In the 1830's a group of people from New York City made a study of the British police system. As a result, in 1844 New York became the first city in the United States to establish a day-and-night police force similar to Peel's.

Before long other cities followed New York's example.

Why are American policemen known as "cops" or "coppers"? Some people believe that the name comes from the eight-pointed copper star once worn by New York policemen. Others believe that the name was taken from the initial letters of the words "constable on patrol."

WHO FIRST MADE BREAD WITH YEAST?

The action of yeast in moist, warm dough is called leavening. The yeast cells convert the starch of the dough into sugar, which they then digest. As they do this they give off carbon dioxide as a waste product. The gas is trapped in the dough, forms larger and larger bubbles, and makes the dough rise.

Wild yeast spores are almost always present in the air and will land naturally on the dough. The first people to discover the value of yeast were the Egyptians. They tried baking with fermented dough and liked the lighter, tastier bread. Bread that rises with the aid of wild yeast, however, may turn out differently each time. This is because different kinds of yeast may fall on it.

The Egyptians discovered a way to control this. Each time they baked they set aside some of the leavened dough to mix with the next batch. In this way they could be sure of using the same kind of yeast.

Around 1000 B.C. Phoenician traders carried the art of making leavened bread to the Greeks, who became the master bakers of antiquity. The Greeks had over 70 different recipes for bread.

The Romans turned baking into a large-scale industry and passed many laws governing the quality of bread. The bakers were so proud of the superior taste of their bread that each baker marked his loaves with his name, just as bakeries put their brand name on the wrappers today.

WHEN DID THE SPORT OF SURFING BEGIN?

Surfing is the sport of riding ocean waves on a long, narrow surfboard. The sport is enjoyed at beaches all over the world and has become so popular that we tend to think of it as a new thing.

But surfing is actually quite old. It apparently originated in the Pacific islands hundreds of years ago. When Captain James Cook discovered Hawaii in 1788, surfing was already a very popular sport among the Hawaiians.

The Hawaiians held surfing contests and the winners who won prizes were acclaimed by the people. The islanders used boards 14 to 18 feet long which were about 150 pounds in weight.

About 1957 a big change took place in surfing that helped make it popular. Lightweight boards began to be used. These boards, which are about 10 feet long and weigh as little as 22 pounds, have made it possible for women and even children to take up surfing. The new boards are generally made of foam plastic, coated with fiberglass and resin. A surfboard is the only special equipment the sport requires.

When riding a wave, surfers stand on the board and maneuver right and left. The surfer must first take his board out past the surf line—the point where the waves begin to break. Kneeling or lying prone on his board, he waits for a set, or series of swells, to form. When the wave he wants to ride comes up behind him, he paddles quickly toward shore with his hands. As the wave moves beneath him, the board first rises with it, then slides down the unbroken front of the wave. Having "caught" the wave, the surfer stands, one foot forward, and steers away from the breaking part of the wave.

HOW DID THE WORDS IN THE ENGLISH LANGUAGE ORIGINATE?

The words of the English language originated in many different ways from many different sources, but Greek and Latin supplied most of the words used in English today. A single Latin word like "manus" ("hand"), for example, is the source of "manufacture," "manicure," "manipulate," "emancipate," and so on.

The Latin word "scribere" ("to write") gives us "scribble," "scripture," "subscription," and many others. The Greek word "autos," meaning "self," gives us "autobiography," "automobile," "autograph," "automatic," and so on.

Many words are formed simply by putting part of a word in front of the root (called a prefix) or adding to the end of a root (a suffix). For example: bi- ("two") makes "bicycle" and "bisect." And: -able ("fitness for") makes "lovable" and "peaceable."

The English language includes words borrowed from many other languages. The English language began early in the Christian era with the dialects of such tribes as the Angles, Jutes, and Saxons. Viking invaders from Scandinavia added to it. And at the time of the Norman Conquest (1066) William the Conqueror's invaders brought many thousands of French and Latin terms into the language.

Later, as English explorers and traders ranged over the world, they borrowed many words from the peoples with whom they traded. For example, from India came such words as "madras," "bungalow," "punch," and "faker." From the Dutch came "freight," "schooner," and "landscape." From Spain and Latin America came "potato," "cargo," "tobacco," and "hurricane." And our language has continued to grow with words from dialects, different peoples, and from new developments in science, sports, and all kinds of activities.

HOW DID WE LEARN TO WRITE?

Nobody knows exactly where and when writing originated. But we do have an idea of how it developed from earliest times.

Man began by making pictures to serve as records of his hunting, wars, and tribal life. Pictures could also be used for messages. A picture of the sun meant a day. Two marks next to the sun meant two days. Such signs are called pictographs.

When civilization developed, this method of writing was speeded up by simplifying the pictures. The Egyptians used a wavy line to mean a body of water. The Chinese used an ear between two doors to mean "listen." Such signs are called ideographs or ideograms.

The ancient Egyptians used a system of signs that we call hieroglyphics. At first it was entirely ideographic. But over the centuries the Egyptians developed a phonetic system as well. This is writing where the signs represent sounds rather than objects or ideas.

As civilization further developed, men needed more and more signs. So they developed a method of spelling words according to sound. For example, in English we would write the "belief" by drawing a bee and a leaf. Such signs are called phonograms, and the writing is syllabic because it uses syllables.

The next stage in the development of writing was the idea of using an alphabet of single letters. Both the ancient Egyptians and the Babylonians knew how to write in the alphabetic way. From their method came the Greek and Latin alphabets which are used today by most people outside of Asia.

WHO INVENTED COMIC BOOKS?

The comic strip is usually found in daily newspapers. It is made up of three or four picture panels telling a story with one or more characters. Comic books are extensions of comic strips into magazines. Each magazine is about one set of characters and the pictures tell a complete story.

While the first newspaper comic strip appeared in 1892, it was not until 1911 that an entire publication was devoted to comics—a comic book. That year the *Chicago American* offered reprints of Bud Fisher's "Mutt and Jeff" in pamphlet form.

The pattern for present-day comics was set much later. In 1935, *New Fun* appeared. It was a 64-page collection of original material in four colors, and was sold at newsstands. In 1938, *Action Comics* appeared, and the *Superman Quarterly Magazine* came out in 1939.

Comic books are not all humorous stories. The types of comic books issued include: adventure, animal, biography, detective, fantasy-mystery, history, humor, military, religion, romance, satire, science-fiction, teen-age, and western.

Some types, such as adventure and humor, sell better, so there are more of them. The popularity of comic books, however, has led all kinds of groups to use comic books to tell a story. Many companies use comic books to tell the story behind a product or the history of their company. Comic books are also published to explain complicated subjects, to dramatize public needs, or to give the history of a particular event. So "comic books" can be as varied as the subject matter and the purpose behind them.

WHAT IS THE ORIGIN OF THE DOG?

All living members of the dog family are descended from a wolflike creature called "Tomarctus." This ancient canine, called "the father of dogs," roamed the earth's forests about 15,000,000 years ago.

Tomarctus itself was descended from a small, weasel-like creature called "Miacis"; it lived some 40,000,000 years ago. This creature was also the distant ancestor of the bears and raccoons. They are the dog's closest living relatives today.

While man admires and lives with the domestic dog, he usually hates and fears such animals as wolves, coyotes, jackals, and foxes. But these are called "wild dogs." Domestic dogs are brothers under the skin to wolves, coyotes, and jackals—the typical wild dogs. All belong to the foremost branch of the dog family, the genus *anis*. All are so closely related that domestic dogs can mate with wolves, coyotes, or jackals, and produce fertile offspring. But they cannot interbreed with foxes. Foxes belong to another branch of the canine family tree.

At some time long ago early man tamed a few wild dogs. These dogs may have been wolf cubs. Or they may have been jackals or some other member of the wild dog family. Man found that these animals could be useful.

As man became more civilized he found that the dog was a good friend and a helpful guard for his home and cattle. In time, different breeds of dogs were developed for special purposes. Dogs with long noses were bred to scent game. Keen-sighted, fast dogs were bred to chase animals. Strong, heavy dogs pulled carts. Other dogs were bred for guard work. In this way the different breeds of dogs we have were developed.

WHEN WERE THE FIRST KEYS MADE?

The ancient Egyptians were the first to use a kind of key to open a door. They had a lock that was made up of a wooden bolt that fitted into a slot. Movable wooden pins known as tumblers were fastened in the top of the slot. When the bolt slid into place, the wooden tumblers dropped into holes cut in the bolt. The bolt was held fast until the tumblers were lifted up with a key.

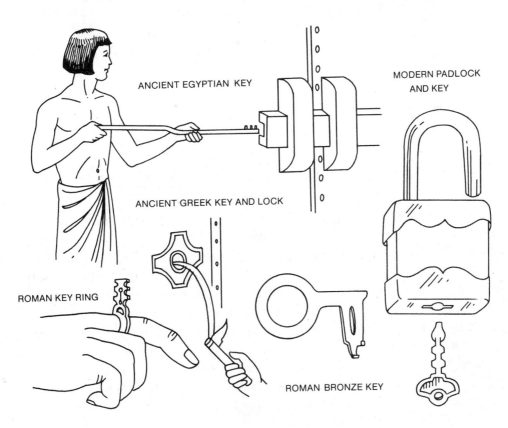

ANCIENT EGYPTIAN KEY

MODERN PADLOCK AND KEY

ANCIENT GREEK KEY AND LOCK

ROMAN KEY RING

ROMAN BRONZE KEY

This first key did not look at all like a key as we know it today. It looked more like a giant-sized toothbrush with pegs instead of bristles on one end. When the key was put in the slot, the pegs went under the tumblers. By raising the key, the tumblers were forced out of the bolt, which was then easily drawn back.

The Egyptian key could only be used on that side of the door where the bolt was placed. The Greeks discovered a way to slide back the bolt from the other side of the door. They slid their key through a hole in the door above the bolt until its tip touched a notch in the bolt on the inside. The Greek key was a curved bar, in shape and size much like a farmer's sickle. Some of these keys were over three feet long and were carried over the shoulder.

The Romans later became the most skillful lockmakers of the ancient world. They made a great improvement in the key. The pegs on the end of the Roman keys were cut in many different shapes. Now a thief had to make a key with pins not only in the right position and of the right length but also of the right shape.

The Romans worked out a small lock that could be carried from place to place. We call such locks padlocks. The small padlock keys were often made in the shape of rings, so they could be worn on a finger.

WHY DO WE HAVE APRIL FOOLS' DAY?

Some customs, holidays, and traditions are very hard to trace to their beginnings. We just do it and can't explain why. April Fools' Day, and how it originated, has been explained in several ways, but no one is quite sure.

First of all, there is a day like our April Fools' Day in nearly all parts of the world. It is a day when practical jokes are played on friends and neighbors, like sending them on foolish errands or tricking them into doing silly things.

It is believed that our April Fools' Day started with the French. When the calendar was reformed, the first nation to adopt the reformed calendar was France. Charles IX ordered, in 1564, that the year should begin with the 1st of January. Until then, New Year's visits and the exchange of New Year's gifts has been associated with the 1st of April.

Now, after Charles issued his decree, all this became associated with the 1st of January. But there were many people who objected to the change and refused to go along with it. The other people made fun of them for this.

They did it this way: they sent them mock gifts, they pretended to be visiting them, they invited them to mock New Year's celebrations—all on the 1st of April. In other words, they were April Fools—people who still felt April 1st was the beginning of the new year. Also, the custom of fooling somebody on this day started with the mock gifts and celebration they had with these people.

WHO SET UP THE ARRANGEMENT OF TYPEWRITER KEYS?

The modern typewriter is a complicated piece of machinery. Development to its present form took many years, and many people contributed to it.

Inventors had been thinking about a machine for writing since early in the 18th century. But it was not until 1867 that the first practical model was built, by Christopher Sholes of Milwaukee, Wisconsin.

Shole's machine was called the Type-Writer. People did not seem too interested in typewriting at first. The popularity of typewriters began to grow, however, in the early 1880's. And changes and improvements kept being introduced all the time.

But the odd arrangement of the typewriter keys has never been improved. This arrangement was the one used by the typewriter's original designer. Some typewriter designers believe that the keys could be arranged more efficiently. They have tried to make such changes in typewriters, but they have not been successful. It seems that the public is used to the keyboard the way it is and wants no change.

The arrangement of the keys is practically the same on all makes of typewriters. This common arrangement of the letters of the alphabet is known as the "universal" keyboard.

Some experts claim that this arrangement is actually a very good one. They say that the letters which occur together most often are placed so that the operator's fingers reach them successively in the most natural way.

WHEN WERE GEMS DISCOVERED?

Nobody knows when man first discovered gems, but he has been fascinated by them since the earliest times. For many thousands of years gems were worn as charms, or amulets, to protect people from demons and diseases. Even today there are people who believe gems have this power.

One of the first written records about gems is found in the Bible. The 28th chapter of Exodus tells of the breastplate worn by the high priest, Aaron. The breastplate was adorned by 12 precious stones.

The ancient Egyptians used gems as ornaments and charms. They were highly skilled in the art of gem engraving, and their writings on precious stones still exist. The Egyptians wore curious amulets, known as scarabs. These were precious stones engraved with the figure of the sacred beetle of Egypt. Those who wore scarabs were believed to have charmed lives.

In ancient times, the various gems were distinguished only by their colors. The name "ruby" was given to all precious stones of a red hue. All green stones were called emeralds. All blue ones were called sapphires.

Later on it was seen that some of the gems were harder than others and endured longer. So it came about that the value of a gem depended not only on its color, brilliance, and rarity, but also on its hardness. For example, diamonds are today considered the most precious of gems because, besides their beauty, they are the hardest of all stones.

All the gems are called precious stones, but in its strict meaning the term "precious" is given only to the four most valuable stones—the diamond, the ruby, the emerald, and the sapphire.

HOW WERE TIME ZONES DECIDED?

Before time zones were set up, there was a great deal of confusion, especially when people had to use railroad timetables. To end this confusion the United States in 1883 began using a system of standard time zones.

In 1884 an international conference was held in Washington, D.C., to set up a system to fit the whole world. The earth was divided into 24 zones, each covering 15 degrees of longitude. This is a natural division, for the earth rotates at the rate of 15 degrees each hour.

Within each zone the time is the same, and the difference between one zone and the next is exactly one hour. Greenwich (London), England, was selected as the starting point. Thus, when it is noon in Greenwich, the time in the next zone eastward is 1 P.M. The time in the next zone westward is 11 A.M. In New York, five zones west of Greenwich, the time is 7 A.M.

The United States is divided into four zones based on the 75th, 90th, 105th, and 120th meridians. The times in these zones are called Eastern, Central, Mountain, and Pacific Standard Time.

On the opposite side of the world from Greenwich is another dividing line, the International Date Line. This line is approximately the 180th meridian. When it is noon at Greenwich it is midnight at the International Date Line. Crossing the line, a person gains or loses a day, depending on whether he is moving east or west.

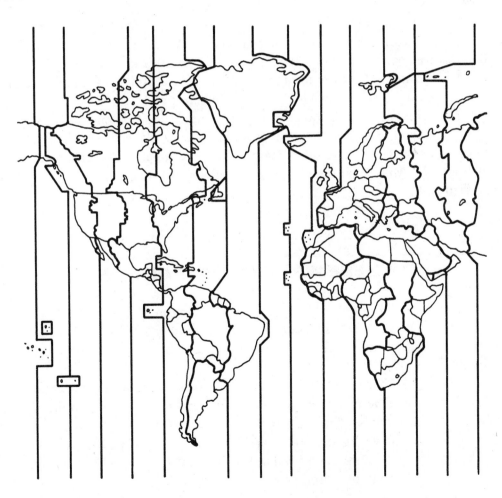

WHEN WERE COWS FIRST USED FOR MILK?

Early records often mention man's use of milk and milk products, and cows were used for milk long before any records were kept.

A temple that was discovered near Babylon has a scene on one of the walls that shows a cow being milked. This temple is thought to be five thousand years old!

Instead of milking cows from the right side, as is done today, the man is milking the cows from behind. The milker sits on a milking stool. Other men are straining the milk into a container on the ground. A third group collects the strained milk in large stone jars. So it seems that the business of getting milk from cows was pretty well organized five thousand years ago.

Today the cow and the goat are the major animals supplying milk for human use. But in various parts of the world people use milk from other animals that are native to their homelands. For example, in Asia the camel, the horse, and the yak are sources of milk. Eskimos and Laplanders use the caribou and the reindeer. Water buffalo are used in India and central Asia. And sheep are used in Europe and Asia to provide milk for human use.

Milk contains several hundred different chemical parts, but it is best known for its calcium, phosphorus, and protein. Since milk is easily digested, the calcium, phosphorus, and other materials can be quickly and effectively used by the body. Milk sugar (lactose) and the major milk protein, casein, are found only in milk.

WHERE WAS RICE FIRST GROWN?

Rice is one of the most important and fascinating foods in the world. Did you know that the Chinese used to greet each other not by saying "How do you do?" but by saying "Have you eaten your rice today?" This was because rice was so important to them.

Nearly half the population of the world lives partly or almost entirely on a rice diet. In some countries of Asia, each person eats from two hundred to four hundred pounds of rice a year.

It is not known for certain where rice was first grown by man, but rice probably originated in southern India. We do know that it has been grown there for many thousands of years.

Rice spread from there eastward to China more than five thousand years ago. It spread westward into Persia and Egypt soon afterward. Rice was not introduced to North America until the 17th century. Although North Americans eat some rice, most of them prefer wheat. At the present time in the United States only about five pounds of rice per person is eaten every year.

Rice with the hulls removed is called brown rice. Brown rice is covered with a brownish outer skin called the bran, in which most of the vitamins and minerals of the rice grain are stored.

Brown rice does not keep as long as white rice, however. Also, most people prefer white, well-milled, polished rice to brown rice. In some countries polished rice is enriched by adding vitamins and minerals.

Rice is used in many ways besides food. Rice flour is used for making glue, starch and in face powders. Wine is made from rice in Japan, China, and India.

WHY WAS THE METRIC SYSTEM INVENTED?

As science began to develop a few hundred years ago, scientists had trouble with measurements. Standards varied from nation to nation and even within one country. So during the 1700's scientists argued for a sensible system of measurement that could be accepted all over the world.

Such a system was invented in France in 1791. The French had other reasons for doing it, too. They were in the middle of a revolution at the time. The leaders of the revolution wanted to get away from all reminders of their hated past. They were therefore willing to set up a new system of measurement.

They began with length. They decided to establish the "meter" (from a Latin word meaning "measure") as a standard. Because of this, the entire system of measurement is called the metric system. Originally they tried to make the meter exactly 1/40,000,000 of the circumference of the earth. But when calculations turned out to be wrong about the earth's circumference, the meter was taken to be the distance between two marks on a platinum-iridium bar. All units of measurement in this system—length, capacity, mass—are linked in some way to the meter.

Actually, the metric system is easy to remember and easy to use. At first, though, people didn't want to change over. In 1840 the French Government had to insist that the people use the metric system or be punished.

Other nations gradually adopted the metric system, and today almost the whole world uses it. The United States is "phasing in" the system today.

WHO INVENTED TRAFFIC SIGNALS?

After the coming of the automobile, the first traffic controllers were foot patrolmen, directing traffic by hand. Then they were given hand-operated traffic lights. It was not until the early 1920's that automatic traffic lights were first used.

But these lights left an important problem unsolved. The amount of traffic passing through an intersection changes at different times of the day.

In 1927 two men patented "traffic-actuated" controllers. These were traffic lights designed to adjust to the amount of traffic passing through an intersection at a given time. One of these lights, invented by Harry Haugh of Yale University, was first installed in New Haven, Connecticut, in April, 1928.

This device worked by means of pressure detectors in the road pavement. A car passing over a detector signaled the "call box" on the light pole, which caused the light to turn green for the approaching vehicle. This type of traffic light, with some changes, is still widely used today.

Charles Adler, also in 1928, invented a traffic light that used a microphone to activate the call box. When a motorist, facing a red light, blew his horn, the microphone transmitted the sound to the call box, which caused the light to change. Today, there are other types of traffic controllers that use sound to change the light.

WHY IS SPEED AT SEA MEASURED IN KNOTS?

When ships first ventured out to sea, they had no sure way of knowing their location. Eventually, this was done by finding the latitude and longitude of the place. Latitude is distance north or south of the equator. Longitude tells how far east or west a place is. It was decided that zero degrees longitude would be the longitude line that goes through Greenwich, England.

To get an idea of their longitude, early ships first calculated how far they had traveled in a certain period of time. They used a "log" to find this out. It was a log of wood, weighted at one end, with the other end fixed to a long piece of rope. The log, thrown over the stern of the ship, floated, and the rope was let out as the ship sailed on. The speed of the ship could be calculated by seeing how much rope had been let out in a given time.

In later years, knots were tied at equal distances along the rope. A sailor counted how many knots passed through his hands in a certain time. This gave the speed of the ship. Sailors came to use the word "knots" to mean the speed of a ship.

Today, a knot has come to mean one nautical, or sea, mile per hour. A nautical mile equals 6076.1 feet, a little more than a land mile. Suppose a ship is sailing at a speed of 15 knots. This means that it is sailing at a speed of 15 nautical miles an hour.

Logs are still used to show how fast a ship is traveling. But today the logs are special metal rods with flat blades around them. As the ship sails through the water, the metal rod rotates and twists the rope round and round. The spinning rope works a device back on the ship that shows the actual speed.

WHEN DID PEOPLE BEGIN TO PIERCE THEIR EARS?

Piercing the ears to wear earrings goes back to prehistoric times. The ancient East Indians, Medes, Persians, Egyptians, Arabians, and Hebrews wore earrings.

Earrings became expensive and artistic ornaments in ancient times. The Etruscans, for example, made gold earrings that took the form of flowers, fruits, vases, shields, rosettes, crescents, peacocks, swans, and so on. The Greeks made beautiful gold earrings, and even put them on statues of the goddesses. In those days, Greek men wore earrings until they reached the age of adolescence.

The ancient Romans copied the Greeks in wearing earrings, and some of the Roman women had very expensive ones made with pearls and jewels. Roman men began to pierce their ears to wear earrings, and this became so popular that in the 3rd century A.D. the Roman emperor issued an edict forbidding men from doing so.

After the Middle Ages, men began to wear earrings in the left ear only. Then the hair styles for men and women changed; and when hair was worn long and over the ears, earrings went out of style. But they came into vogue again in the 15th and 16th centuries.

Earrings for women have been popular ever since that time. At one time, doctors said that it was good for ears to be pierced, but they no longer believe that it helps the ear.

WHO WERE THE FIRST PEOPLE TO MAKE MUMMIES?

The ancient Egyptians believed in life after death. They thought of the soul as a bird with a human face that could fly around by day but must return to the tomb at night for fear of evil spirits. The body was therefore preserved so that the soul could recognize it and know which tomb to enter. This is where the word "mummy" comes from. It is Arabic and means a body preserved by wax or tar.

Most mummies were not made using wax or tar. The body was treated with salts. Salts, put inside the body, together with the dryness of the desert air, took out the moisture. When the body had been dried out, it was bathed, rubbed with resin from pine trees, and wrapped in hundreds of yards of linen.

Before about 3000 B.C. the Egyptians buried their dead in a curled-up position in the hot sand of the desert. The sand preserved the bodies. Later, important persons were buried in tombs cut from rock and in magnificent pyramids. But the pyramids and rock tombs were not so dry as the desert sand. This made it necessary to develop the art of mummification.

About 1500 B.C., mummies were given a plaster covering, shaped like a body and elaborately painted. Soon the coffins took the same shape and were decorated. Beards were added to some of the mummy cases. The beard in ancient Egypt was the sign of a god or king. Adding a beard showed that the dead man expected to live in very high company in the afterworld.

The Egyptians also believed that certain animals were sacred. These animals were also mummified and buried in animal cemeteries.

WHY DO WE HAVE CHRISTMAS TREES?

The custom came from Germany and dates to a time when primitive people revered trees—particularly evergreens. These trees did not die or fade in winter and seemed to be a sign of immortality. The Christians changed the custom into one honoring Christ.

The northern peoples of Denmark, Sweden, and Norway, where the forests are plentiful, adopted the custom of bringing small trees into their homes at Christmastime.

Trees were not used in English homes until a German prince, Albert of Saxe-Coburg-Gotha, married Queen Victoria. Prince Albert had the first decorated Christmas tree set up at Windsor Castle in 1841.

The first Christmas trees in the New World were introduced by Hessian soldiers in 1776, during the American Revolution. Later on, German immigrants brought the tradition into wider use in the United States.

Many other Christmas decorations used today were once pagan symbols. The Romans used flowers and leafy boughs in their rites. Records show that the Saxons used holly, ivy, and bay in their religious observances. The Druids gave the world the tradition of hanging mistletoe in the house. (Ancient Celtic priests believed the plant to be a sign of hope and peace.)

WHY WAS WASHINGTON D.C. MADE THE CAPITAL OF THE UNITED STATES?

After the American Revolution the United States needed a capital city. The selection of the site resulted from a compromise. Various cities and sections of the country wanted the honor of being the nation's capital.

It was finally decided to create a new city. Congress passed a bill in 1790 giving permission for a site to be chosen. It was to be somewhere near the Potomac River and not over ten miles square. The ten-mile square section of the land was to be called the District of Columbia, after Christopher Columbus; and the city to be built on it was to be named Washington, in honor of the country's first president.

In 1791 George Washington chose the place where the city now stands. He thought it was a good location because the Potomac River was deep enough for ships to come as far as the city.

The land was given to the federal government by the states of Maryland and Virginia. About 64 square miles were given by Maryland and about 36 square miles by Virginia. Later, in 1846, the land given by Virginia was returned to the state at her request.

President Washington chose a brilliant French engineer and architect, Major Pierre L'Enfant, to design the new city. The plan called for broad avenues lined with trees, beautiful government buildings, and monuments to honor great men.

By 1800 the president's house was nearly completed. The Capitol was built on a hill, renamed Capitol Hill, for the building in which Congress was to meet. In 1800 President John Adams and other members of the government moved to the new federal city, Washington, D.C.

HOW DID THE NAME "UNCLE SAM" ORIGINATE?

"Uncle Sam," of course, stands for the United States. What is hard to believe is that this nickname arose quite by accident, and there actually was a man called "Uncle Sam"—and that most people never heard of him!

There was a man called "Uncle Sam" Wilson. He was born in Arlington, Mass., Sept. 13, 1766. His father and older brothers fought in the American

Revolution. Sam himself enlisted at the age of 14 and served until the end of the war. He moved to Troy, N. Y., and began a meat-packing business.

On Oct. 2, 1812, a group of visitors came to his plant. One of them, Governor Daniel D. Tompkins of New York, asked what the initials "EA-US" on the barrels of meat stood for. A workman replied the "EA" stood for the contractor for whom Wilson worked, Elbert Anderson. And he added jokingly that the "US" (actually an abbreviation for United States) stood for "Uncle Sam" Wilson.

A story of this incident appeared in the May 12, 1830 issue of the New York *Gazette and General Advertiser*. Since Wilson was a popular man, and was an example of a hard-working and patriotic American, the idea of "Uncle Sam" as a name for this kind of man caught on quickly.

By the end of the War of 1812, "Uncle Sam" had come to symbolize the character of the nation and the government. In 1961 Congress adopted a resolution saluting "Uncle Sam" Wilson of Troy, N. Y., as the "progenitor of America's national symbol."

HOW OLD IS THE GAME OF CHECKERS?

Two of the oldest games played by man are chess and checkers. They are related in some ways, but since checkers is simpler in form it is assumed that it came first.

Checkers was played in the early history of Egypt, which means it's at least five thousand years old. Plato and Homer mentioned the game of checkers in their works, so it was known in ancient Greece. The Romans are believed to have taken the game from the Greeks.

The earliest records of the game seem to indicate that the kind of board used was similar to what we use today, and that it was played with twelve men on each side.

The first book on checkers was published in Spain in 1547. In 1620 another book of checkers was published in Spain that contained sample games and traps that would still be useful to know today. It is believed that the Spaniards may have learned about checkers from the Moors, who brought it from Arabia.

In England (where it is called "draughts"), the first book on checkers appeared in 1756. In 1800 another book by a man called Joshua Sturges became a guidebook for playing checkers that everyone followed for more than 50 years.

Today, checkers is played by millions of people all over the world. It is also recognized by educators as a good way to help people develop foresight, judgment, and concentration.

WHEN WERE THE FIRST MUSEUMS OPENED?

Museums are places where collections of objects are preserved and displayed. The objects may be anything found in nature or made by man. There are museums devoted to art, science, history, industry, and technology.

The word "museum" comes from the Greek word *mousion,* meaning "temple of the Muses." The Muses were goddesses of the arts. One of the first institutions to be called a mouseion was founded in Alexandria, Egypt, in the 3rd century B.C.

The aim of the Museum of Alexandria, as it was known, was to collect information from everywhere that could be of interest to scholars. Scholars lived and did their research there. The museum displayed a collection of objects of art and curiosities that included statues, instruments used in astronomy and surgery, elephant tusks, and hides of unusual animals.

There were many collections that might be called museums between that time and the 19th century, but they belonged to princes and noble families and were not established for the benefit of the people. Even the British Museum, which was founded in the middle of the 18th century, admitted few people.

It took the French Revolution to open the doors of French museums to everyone. In 1793, during the Revolution, the Republican Government made the Louvre in Paris a national museum.

In the 19th century, for the first time, buildings were specially designed as museums. One of the first buildings in Europe planned as a museum was the Altes Museum in Berlin, Germany. It was constructed in 1830.

WHO INVENTED THE VIOLIN?

The violin is known as the queen of instruments. Of the more than one hundred musicians in a great orchestra, over thirty are violinists. The violin's high rank is due to the beauty of its tone and its wide range of expression.

The violin took many centuries to develop. Its history begins in India, where the use of a bow to play stringed instruments was probably invented. During the early Middle Ages in Europe various stringed instruments were played with a bow.

One of these was the vielle, which was probably introduced to Europe through the Balkan Peninsula in the 10th century. Like the violin, the vielle was held against the player's shoulder.

Later the vielle was changed through the influence of the rebec. This was an Arabic instrument that spread from Spain to the rest of Europe. By combining the sturdy body of the vielle with the clever arrangement of the pegs in the rebec, a new group of instruments was born.

The violin received its basic form between 1550 and 1600. Since that time it has changed only in small ways. The most successful violins were made in the 17th and 18th centuries.

Italy produced outstanding families of violin-makers. Probably the greatest of these was Antonio Stradivari (1644-1737). Stradivari is called the master of all masters. He developed a larger, flatter type of violin than had been made before, which gave it more tone power.

Stradivari is said to have built 1,116 instruments. Of these, 540 "Strad" violins are known to us. Most of them have nicknames, such as the Viotti or the Vieuxtemps, after the famous violinists who played them.

WHO INVENTED MUSICAL NOTES?

For a very long time music was not written down. It was sung or played from memory. As it was passed on from person to person, many changes crept into the tunes. A way of writing music down was needed so that it would be sung or played exactly as it had been composed. The method that man developed for writing music is called notation.

The system of musical notation generally used today in the Western world is the result of centuries of development—from about the end of the 9th century to the early 1700's. This development began in the cathedrals and monasteries of the Roman Catholic Church.

Since many of the Church's services were sung, they were sung from memory. Toward the end of the 9th century dots and dashes and little squiggles were written over the words in the service books. These signs, called neumes, showed the direction in which the melody should go. But they were still very vague.

About A.D. 900 the music was made a little easier to read. The neumes were written at certain distances above or below the horizontal red line (representing the note F) to show how high or low the note should be sung.

Then the staff was invented by a monk called Guido d'Arezzo. This was made of four lines. A method of notation that made it possible to show the length of each note was developed in the 13th and 14th centuries. Notes took new shapes and stems were added to some notes according to their length. By the 1600's the notes had become round and musical notation began to look the way it does today.

WHY DO SOLDIERS SALUTE?

What is a salute? It is a gesture of respect to a person of superior rank. It is formalized, that is, it is done in a certain way every time.

Salutes of all kinds have existed in all periods of history and in all cultures. The form of salute has varied. In some cases it meant bowing, in others it meant kneeling, or lying on the ground, or various gestures of the hand and arm. The individual military salute that a soldier gives—raising the right hand to the forehead or to the hat brim or visor—was developed quite recently in history.

Until the end of the 18th century the way junior officers saluted superiors and soldiers saluted officers was to doff the hat. In fact, civilians still do this as a gesture of respect. And this custom probably goes back to the days when a knight would raise his helmet's visor or uncover his head before a lord.

The change from taking off the hat to just raising the hand in a salute, took place for a very practical reason. When soldiers fired their muskets, black powder would settle on their hands and make them very grimy. If they then had to use their grimy hands to take off their hats in a salute, it would ruin the hats. So at the end of the 18th century the change was made to the hand salute.

An officer or soldier carrying a sword or saber at the shoulder, whether mounted or on foot, salutes by bringing the hilt to his mouth, then extending the point to the right and downward. This form of salute dates back to the Middle Ages when knights, in a religious gesture, kissed the hilts of their swords as symbolic of the cross of Christ. It was then a form of oath-taking.

WHEN DID ATHLETICS BEGIN?

If we go back far enough, athletics probably began with religion. Primitive men worshipped their gods by performing certain dances. These dances imitated the actions of fighting and hunting. Later on, these dances were performed simply for the pleasure they gave—and they were actually a form of athletics.

The Egyptians had some form of athletic sports about four thousand years ago. But athletics as we know it really began with the Greeks. The first recorded Olympic games of the Greeks took place in the year 776 B.C.

Today, we imagine that sports activities play an important part in our lives. But it cannot compare to how important athletics were to the ancient Greeks. Every boy was trained in running, jumping, and wrestling, while he was still at school. A man was supposed to be good at athletics until he was well past middle age.

The ideal of the Greeks was to have a sound mind in a healthy body. So they didn't admire men who were just athletes, nor men who were just brilliant but couldn't participate in sports. But they also had professional athletes, especially in boxing and wrestling.

The Greeks had many athletic festivals, but the oldest and most important were the Olympic games. Only young men of pure Greek descent who had undergone ten months' training could compete. At first the games were just contests in running and jumping. But later on they added wrestling, boxing, discus and javelin throwing, and chariot races.

WHO INVENTED INDOOR PLUMBING?

By indoor plumbing we generally mean a system that consists of two parts. There is a system of pipes and valves that brings the water from a large pipe (water main) under the street into the house and to the various rooms. There is also a drainage system of pipes through which waste liquids are taken from the house and fed into a sewer pipe in the street.

The first "plumbing" system that we know about goes back about 4,000 years. Archeologists doing excavations on Crete, an island in the Mediterranean Sea, uncovered a 4,000-year-old palace that had a water and drainage system.

The water system was formed by conduits—stone channels through which water flows. The cisterns of the conduits collected water that fell as rain or flowed down from the hills. The water was carried by the conduits into vertical shafts and from the shafts to bathrooms and toilets.

Waste water was carried away by pipes made of terra-cotta, a form of baked clay. Amazingly enough, these terra-cotta pipes were designed so that they could be installed easily. One end of each pipe was made so it would fit into the next, and the pipes were fastened together with cementing clay.

The first people to use pipes made of lead were the Romans. They called the craftsman who installed pipes a "plumbarius," meaning "worker in lead." This is the origin of the English words "plumber" and "plumbing."

While lead is still used in some kinds of pipes today, other materials used are steel, copper, brass, cast iron, concrete, and plastic.

WHEN WAS JEWELRY FIRST WORN?

Jewelry can be made from many different kinds of materials. But we usually think of it as precious jewelry, made of the rarest and most beautiful metals and gemstones.

Gold is the oldest precious metal used in jewelry. The use of it dates back to the earliest Egyptians. In fact, more than four thousand years ago, the Egyp-

ANCIENT EGYPTIAN RING

ANCIENT GREEK GOLD DECORATION

ANCIENT ROMAN NECKLACE

GEMS

EARLY MIDDLE AGES RING

ETRUSCAN BROOCH

tians were making beautiful jewelry out of gold, silver, enamel, turquoise and other gemstones. They wore rings, earrings, and brooches, just as we do now. They also wore heavy jeweled collars, breastplates, and headdresses.

To the ancient Greeks the beauty of a piece of jewelry was as important as the value of the materials used to make it. Fine threads of gold were shaped to look like butterflies or grasshoppers. The Greeks also liked cameos. Jasper, amber, and coral were among their favorite gemstones.

The most beautifully made jewelry in history was made by the Etruscans, who lived in northern Italy. They designed jewelry in intricate patterns and made it with great skill. Instead of a shiny surface, their gold jewelry had a grainy surface, as if fine gold powder has been evenly sprinkled on it.

The Romans wore very elaborate jewelry, designed to show off their wealth. Both men and women wore large gemstones. They especially liked pearls and emeralds. The Romans loaded their fingers, sometimes all their fingers, with rings.

During the Middle Ages most of the jewelry craftsmen were monks. The monks devoted their energy to making religious decorations for the churches. Guilds of jewelry makers began after the 9th century. By 1327, goldsmiths had formed their own association in London.

CHAPTER 2
OUR WORLD

HOW DOES WATER PUT OUT A FIRE?

Let's start with what it takes to make a fire. Three things are needed for a fire. The first is a fuel, such as wood or paper or alcohol or gas.

Secondly, oxygen is needed. The fuel combines rapidly with oxygen. When wood burns in bonfires or gas burns in stoves, the fuel combines rapidly with oxygen in the air.

The third thing needed is heat. Paper or wood that is simply exposed to air does not catch fire. Usually a burning match is applied to paper to make it catch fire. When the paper becomes hot enough, oxygen can begin to combine freely with it. The paper then bursts into flames.

There are three main ways in which a fire can be put out. In each, one of the three things needed for burning is removed. The first way is to remove some of the fuel. A second way of putting out a fire is to keep oxygen from getting to it. If there is no oxygen supply, the fire goes out. For example, a fire cannot burn in carbon dioxide. Some fire extinguishers blanket a fire with carbon dioxide. The oxygen is thus blocked from the fire.

A third way to put fires out is to remove heat from the fire. That is why water is sprayed on fires. The water absorbs heat from the burning materials and lowers their temperature. Once the temperature drops below the kindling temperature, the fuels stop burning.

Some fires cannot be put out with water. For example: oil and grease float on water. If you try to put out an oil fire—such as a burning pan of cooking oil—with water, the flaming oil will come to the top of the water and continue to burn.

HOW ARE AMENDMENTS ADDED TO
THE CONSTITUTION?

The Constitution of the United States has grown with the needs of the American people. One of the ways this has happened is through amendments. An amendment means that the words that make up the Constitution can be changed.

When two-thirds of the members of Congress agree on an amendment, the amendment may then be given to the states for their approval. The states may consider the matter either through their legislatures or through special conventions. Congress decides which. And when three-quarters of the states have ratified an amendment, the amendment is in force and the Secretary of State announces the fact.

The first ten amendments, the Bill of Rights, were really unfinished business of the Constitutional Convention. In other words, they were part of the creation of the Constitution. Amendments Eleven and Twelve were also added in that way.

After a long period with no amendments, Thirteen abolished slavery. Fourteen further protected the rights of citizens, and Fifteen granted equal voting rights regardless of race or color. Sixteen permitted Congress to levy an income tax. Seventeen called for the election of senators by the people instead of by state legislatures.

Eighteen outlawed alcoholic drinks—and was repealed by amendment Twenty-one in 1933. The Nineteenth amendment gave women the right to vote. Twenty changed the terms of office of the president, vice-president, and Congress. Twenty-two limits presidents to two terms. Twenty-three gives the presidential vote to the District of Columbia. Twenty-four bars the poll tax as a requirement for voters in federal elections. And Twenty-five covers presidential disability.

HOW DOES THE SOIL HELP PLANTS GROW?

Soil is a mixture of organic and inorganic materials. The organic part consists of living things and the remains of once-living things. The inorganic part is made up of particles of rocks and minerals.

The decaying organic matter in soil is called humus. Humus separates otherwise tightly packed rock particles, thus allowing more air and water to enter the soil. Humus also provides food for bacteria and other micro-organisms in soil. These micro-organisms decay, or break down, dead organic matter, forming substances that plants can use. So humus is very important to the fertility of the soil, or helping plants grow.

Many kinds of animals live in the soil. The body wastes of these animals enrich the soil. Earthworms are important, too. They turn over the soil, and improve it in many ways. Micro-organisms present in the soil feed on particles of organic matter. This breaks the organic material into minerals, gases, and liquids. These decay products are broken down still further and result in new combinations of the basic elements. Plants can then use the substances for growth.

There are ten elements that all plants need to grow. Three of these, oxygen, hydrogen, and carbon, are present in either air or water or in both. The others are obtained from the soil by the plants. They are: nitrogen, phosphorus, potassium, calcium, magnesium, iron, and sulfur.

HOW DO SEEDS GROW?

Each seed is like a tiny package of plant life. It contains a tiny new plant and food to nourish it. You can see the plant and its food if you split a large seed, like a bean, in half.

You will see that it is made of two pale, thick leaves, called cotyledons. These are filled with starch for the developing plant. If you look carefully, you will see a tiny white sprout at one end between the cotyledons. This is the future bean plant. Some plants have only one cotyledon.

Some seeds germinate, or sprout, as soon as they fall from the plant, but most need a resting period of several months. The root appears first. Then a leafy shoot pushes upward.

Seeds enclosed in fleshy fruits, such as apples and tomatoes, do not sprout until they have been removed from the fruit. This is because the fruit contains substances that prevent sprouting.

The tiny new plant in the seed, called the embryo, has an upper part called the plumule. This grows into stems and leaves. The rest of the embryo is the hypocotyl, a very short stem that produces a root at its lower end.

Seeds sprout into new plants when conditions are favorable. The conditions that make seeds sprout are warmth, abundant moisture, and an adequate oxygen supply. Given these conditions, the food stored in the cotyledons passes to the growing regions of the embryo. The embryo bursts through the seed coat and emerges as a young plant that gradually comes to look like the parent plant.

WHAT ARE DIATOMS?

Diatoms are tiny one-celled plants. They are found by the billions and billions in all the waters all over the earth.

The largest diatoms are barely visible to the naked eye and the smallest are less than a thousandth of an inch long. Yet even though they are so tiny, each of them builds for itself a stone shelter hard as granite. There are more than 10,000 species of diatoms, and they have many shapes.

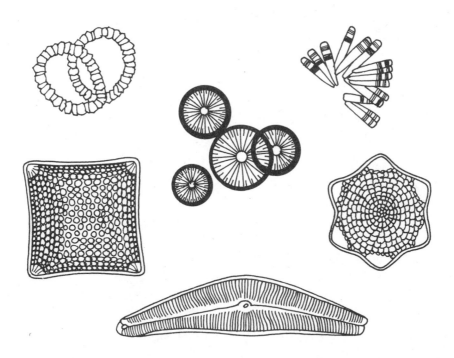

A diatom shelter consists of two shells or valves, one fitting over the other like the top and bottom of a box, and held together along the edges by a girdle. Inside lies the living plant.

Most diatoms float about in the water or fasten themselves with a sort of jelly to stones or larger water plants. A few are able to swim slowly from place to place, but how they propel themselves is not clearly understood.

Diatoms usually reproduce by splitting in two. The interior living cell divides, the valves separate, and each half grows a new valve on its exposed surface.

Diatoms are very important to us. Together with certain other tiny forms, they are the main plant life of the oceans. While alive, they change nutrient materials that are dissolved in the water into organic substance, and so they are a source of food for all kinds of creatures in the sea, even including fish and whales. The oil which they produce is rich in vitamins and is accumulated in fish livers, from which commercial vitamins are produced.

WHEN DID PLANTS APPEAR ON EARTH?

Scientists believe that when life first began on earth more than two billion years ago, the only plant life was in the sea. The land was bare and lifeless.

Then, about 425,000,000 years ago, a few small green plants appeared on land. They probably developed from certain kinds of green sea weeds (algae). The first land plants looked very much like the mosses, liverworts, and hornworts you can see growing in damp, shady places.

About 400,000,000 years ago more complicated plants existed. These resembled modern ferns, horsetails, and club mosses. Ferns were the first plants to have roots, stems, and leaves.

By the time the first dinosaurs walked the earth, vast forests of seed ferns, ginkgoes, cycads, and cordaitales stretched across the land. These were the first trees to reproduce by means of seeds.

Pines and other conifers (cone-bearing trees) developed somewhat later, 300,000,000 years ago. This group includes many familiar trees, such as pines, firs, spruces, cedars, hemlocks, and redwoods. All of these trees bear their seeds on cones.

The first flowering plants developed about 150,000,000 years ago. Their well-protected seeds gave them a great advantage over plants with more exposed seeds, and they increased in numbers and kinds. Today flowering plants are found almost everywhere.

WHO CARVED THE FACES ON MOUNT RUSHMORE?

In the Black Hills of South Dakota, about 25 miles southwest of Rapid City, is one of the most impressive sights to be seen anywhere. It is Mount Rushmore National Memorial.

It honors four American presidents: George Washington, Thomas Jefferson, Abraham Lincoln, and Theodore Roosevelt. Giant likenesses of the four are sculptured into the granite of Mount Rushmore, which is 5,725 feet high. Each face is about 60 feet from chin to forehead, which, by the way, is twice as high as the great Sphinx.

The work was designed by the American sculptor Gutzon Borglum. Borglum was a man who was interested in producing American art, art that related to this country and its history. Well-known works done by him include the colossal head of Lincoln in Washington, D.C., the statue of General Sheridan, and the figures of the twelve apostles for the Cathedral of St. John the Divine, New York City.

Borglum began his work on Mount Rushmore in August, 1927. The first figure, that of Washington, was dedicated on July 4, 1930. After Borglum died on March 6, 1941, work on the memorial continued until October under the direction of his son, Lincoln. But the last sculpture, of Roosevelt, was never quite completed.

Fourteen years passed between the beginning of the project and its termination. But only about six and one-half of these were spent in actual work. The lapses of time without any work being done were due to bad weather and a lack of funds.

The total cost was just under $1 million. The federal government gave 84 percent of this; the rest came from private donations.

WHEN WAS THE GREAT SPHINX BUILT?

One of the greatest "wonders" that still survives from an ancient civilization is the Great Sphinx at Giza, in Egypt. A sphinx is a mythical animal that has the head of a human and the body of a lion.

The sphinx became part of Egyptian religion and many sphinxes were made, but the most famous and the oldest is the Great Sphinx. This sphinx was built in the 26th century B.C. The face had the features of the king at that time, King Khafre, so that his people could worship him in this special form.

It is carved from a natural bluff of rock that lies in the center of a large quarry. The body and the head are carved right from the rock, while the outstretched paws are added in masonry. The figure was originally covered with painted plaster, and there are still some traces of this.

While we can still see and admire the Great Sphinx, it is quite different now than it was originally because of all the damage it has suffered. Drifting sand has caused a great deal of erosion and created a kind of ripple effect on the body.

It has also been injured by humans. In 1380 a ruler of Egypt did great damage to the face. At one time the monument was used as a target for guns.

The Great Sphinx is 66 feet high, its length is 240 feet. The nose is 5 feet 7 inches and the mouth 7 feet 7 inches in length. The face is 13 feet 8 inches wide.

ARE THE CONTINENTS MOVING?

The theory that the continents have moved or drifted about ("continental drift") was first advanced by a German scientist, Alfred Wegener, in 1912.

He pointed out that coal was present all over the northern hemisphere, yet coal forms from plants growing in tropical forests. And among other things, he said the west coast of Africa and the east coast of South America matched so well that they looked as if they had been torn apart.

Wegener thought all the continents had at first been together in one great land mass. Then they had drifted apart to their present location. Most geologists didn't agree with him because no one could think of any way by which continents would move about.

Then scientists began to suggest ways in which this could happen. One was that heat from the interior of the earth creates convection currents that make the continents move. Other scientists now think that the ocean floor is being pulled apart by currents in the mantle of the earth's crust.

So there is no agreement on the subject. Earth scientists tend to accept the idea; those who study under-ocean geology are more ready to accept it. If all geologists were to accept the theory that the continents have drifted, and may still be moving, a great revolution in our ideas on earth science will have to take place.

Science would have to come up with new answers about our climate, about how plants and animals evolved, about how mountains were built, and many more areas.

WHAT IS MAGMA?

Inside the earth it is very hot. This great heat melts some rock material that is there and makes it liquid rock. Liquid rock lies in huge underground pockets. This liquid underground rock is called magma.

Magma is lighter in weight than the colder, hard rocks around it. So it is slowly pushed upward by the pressure of the rock around it. In many places the magma never does reach the surface but slowly cools and hardens underground.

It takes many thousands of years for magma to harden into rock. In other places the cold, hard rocks near the surface cannot withstand the pressure of the magma beneath them. They crack a little bit and the magma rises up along the cracks.

Magma often remains hot enough to stay in liquid form until it reaches the surface of the earth. It then flows through the cracks and spreads out on the ground. Magma that reaches the surface of the earth is called lava.

Magma usually starts cooling while it is still being pushed upward. As the magma slowly rises, certain minerals in it grow into big crystals sooner than the other minerals do. The crystals float in the magma. When this magma reaches the surface of the earth, the liquid rock turns to a solid in a short time. The big crystals carried in the liquid are "frozen" into the fine-grained lava rock. The whole rock is then made of many large crystals embedded in a very fine-grained rock, such as basalt. Such a rock is called porphyry. It is very attractive when polished and is often used as a building stone.

WHY IS LAVA HOT?

The center of the earth is a very hot place. If we could dig down thirty miles into the earth, the temperature would be about 2,200 degrees Fahrenheit. At the core or center of the earth the temperature may be about 10,000 degrees Fahrenheit. At such temperatures, rock exists in a molten form.

Lava is the molten rock, mixed with steam and gas, that is forced out of the interior of the earth. It comes from the center of the earth through cracks in the solid surface.

Sometimes the crack may be a rounded hole. When the lava comes out, it spreads out into a kind of round puddle and cools into rock. If more lava is forced out later, it flows over the first deposit and makes it a little higher. As this continues to happen, layer after layer is built up and there is finally a mountain of rock which we call a volcano.

When a flow of lava occurs and spreads over the land, it destroys everything in its path. This is because it is a heavy stream of molten rock with a temperature of 2,000 to 3,000 degrees Fahrenheit.

Cities that are close to volcanoes are always in danger of being destroyed by such a flow of lava. Sometimes a very long period goes by without this happening, and people assume they are now safe forever. Then suddenly the flow of lava begins again.

This happened two thousand years ago to a Roman city in Italy, called Pompeii. It was buried completely under the flow of lava from the famous volcano, Mount Vesuvius.

WHY DOES THE MOON HAVE DIFFERENT SHAPES?

The moon circles the earth in an orbit that takes about one month to complete. It also spins, or rotates, on its axis, and it takes 27 days, 7 hours, and 43 minutes to make one rotation. Because the orbit and the rotation take about the same amount of time, the moon always keeps the same side facing the earth.

The moon does not shine with its own light the way the sun does. It only seems to shine, because it reflects the sun's light. As the moon travels around the earth different parts of it are lighted up by the sun.

Sometimes you see the whole visible face of the moon lighted up, and at other times you see only a part of the moon's face lighted up. This is what makes the moon look as though it were changing shape in the sky. These changes are called phases of the moon—and it only means we are seeing different parts of the moon.

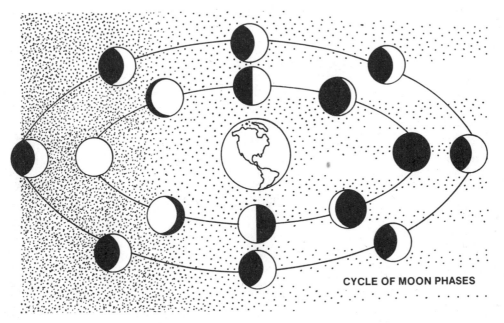

CYCLE OF MOON PHASES

The cycle of phases begins with a new moon. This is when the moon is between the earth and the sun. A new moon is not visible. Then the side of the moon facing the earth begins to be lighted up by the sun. The lighted part looks like a thin curved slice of a circle. This is called a crescent moon.

The sunlit part of the moon grows larger until it becomes a half-circle. This is called the first quarter. When the whole face of the moon is lighted by the sun we call it a full moon. Then the moon's face becomes less and less lit, and we reach the last quarter. The cycle ends with a crescent moon that changes to the next new moon. The whole cycle, from one new moon to the next new moon, lasts just over 29½ days.

WHY IS THERE NO LIFE ON THE MOON?

Now that man has actually explored the surface of the moon, he has learned many new things about it. But one thing man knew before he ever reached the moon was that there was no life on it.

There is no atmosphere on the moon. Astronomers knew this because there is no twilight on the moon. On earth darkness comes gradually because the air reflects the sun's light even after the sun sets. On the moon, one moment there is sunlight, the next moment night has arrived.

The lack of air means that the moon is not protected from any of the sun's rays. The sun sends out heat and light radiation. Life on earth depends on heat and light.

But the sun also sends out dangerous kinds of radiation. The earth's atmosphere protects us from most of them. On the moon, however, there is no atmosphere to stop the radiations. All the sun's rays beat down on the surface of the moon.

Because there is no atmosphere, the moon's surface is either extremely hot or extremely cold. As the moon rotates, the side of it that is lighted up by the sun becomes very hot. The temperature there reaches more than 300 degrees Fahrenheit. This is hotter than boiling water. The hot lunar day lasts two weeks.

It is followed by a night that is also two weeks long. At night the temperature drops to 260 degrees below zero. This is more than twice as cold as temperatures reached at the earth's South Pole.

Under these conditions, no form of life that we know of here on earth could exist on the moon.

DO OTHER PLANETS MOVE LIKE THE EARTH?

The earth moves in two ways. It travels around the sun in a fixed path called an orbit. The time it takes to do this is called a year. The earth also rotates on its axis. The time it takes to do this is called a day. The other planets also orbit the sun and also rotate, but at speeds different from the earth's.

The earth travels around the sun at an average distance of about 93,000,000 miles and takes slightly more than 365 days to make one orbit. It takes a little less than 24 hours to rotate once on its axis. Now let's consider the other planets. Mercury's average distance from the sun is about 36,000,000 miles and it takes 88 earth days to complete one trip around the sun. It is believed that Mercury rotates once every 58 or 59 days.

Venus, about 67,200,000 miles from the sun, takes about 225 days to make one trip around the sun. It is believed that Venus takes 243 days to rotate just once—and this planet rotates backward! In other words, on Venus you would find the planet turning from east to west.

Mars, an average distance of 141,600,000 miles from the sun, takes about 687 days for one orbit, but rotates nearly as fast as the earth. Jupiter, 483,300,000 miles from the sun, takes about 11.9 earth years to complete one orbit, but takes less than ten hours to rotate once. Saturn, 886,200,000 miles from the sun, takes nearly 29½ earth years for one orbit, but only about ten hours to turn once on its axis.

Uranus, 1,783,000,000 miles from the sun, completes an orbit in 84 years. And Neptune, 2,794,000,000 miles from the sun, takes almost 165 earth years to complete one orbit.

WHAT MAKES A BEAUTIFUL SUNSET?

The sun itself has nothing to do with creating a beautiful sunset. And strangely enough, one of the things that helps create that effect is the dust in the air. In fact, dust particles help make the sky blue and give us those red sunsets.

The sun's white light is actually made up of all the colors of the rainbow. Each color has its own wavelength. Violet has the shortest wavelength, red has the longest.

At sunset the sun is near the horizon. We see it then through a much thicker layer of dust and air. All these particles change the direction of more and more short-wave light from the sun. Only the longer wavelengths—red and orange—come through directly.

Violets, blues, and greens are scattered out of the direct beam; they mix and make a gray twilight glow all around the sky. The disk of the sun itself looks red. Sometimes there are clouds in the part of the sky where we see the sun. They reflect this red light and we see a blazing sunset.

Violet and blue light waves are scattered more than the longer red ones. The scattered violet and blue light bounces from particle to particle in the atmosphere, thus spreading light through the whole sky. Since our eyes see blue light more easily than violet, the sky looks blue to us. This, of course, is what happens during the day.

By the way, the redness of a sunset depends on the kind of particles in the air that will be scattering the sun's light. Tiny water droplets are especially effective at this, which is why certain cloud formations appear so red at sunset.

WHAT IS THE DIFFERENCE BETWEEN TOADSTOOLS AND MUSHROOMS?

The answer is, there is no difference! In fact, scientifically speaking, there is no such thing as a "toadstool." Many people call poisonous mushrooms "toadstools." But a botanist never uses that term at all, and there is no difference between a mushroom and what is called a toadstool.

There are a great many other ideas about mushrooms that people have which are completely wrong. The kinds of mushrooms which are poisonous are quite few. But these few are deadly. So no one should ever eat or even taste a mushroom unless he is certain that it is wholesome.

But the "tests" that some people believe in for detecting poisonous mushrooms are worthless. For example, it is not correct that all mushrooms with umbrella-shaped caps are poisonous. It is not true that poisonous mushrooms when cooling will blacken a silver spoon if they are stirred with it.

The poisonous mushrooms contain a poison so powerful that to eat them is almost certain death. There is a story that the Emperor Nero once killed off a whole party of guests by feeding them poisonous mushrooms. The best thing to do is to eat only the mushrooms you buy in stores—and not pick your own.

Mushrooms are fungi. Like other fungi, they lack the green coloring matter called chlorophyll without which a plant cannot manufacture food for itself. They must grow near, and depend for food on, plants that have this green coloring matter. Mushrooms are very delicate plants. They consist chiefly of water, which is why most of them cannot bear hot dry winds or the summer sun.

HOW WAS PETROLEUM FORMED IN THE EARTH?

Petroleum is believed to have been formed from the remains of ancient living things. Millions of years ago many land areas of today were underwater. The sun shone on these waters and the living things in them.

Marine plants and animals stored the sun's energy in their bodies. As they died, their remains sank to the bottom and were covered by sediments (tiny particles of rock and soil).

While organic remains of these animals and plants settled under layers of sand and mud, chemicals and bacteria were at work. How these agents actually formed gas and oil from the fats and oils of sea life is uncertain. But over long periods of time tiny oil droplets were formed. . .or what we call petroleum.

Later on, the layers of muds and clays became rocks of sandstone and limestone. These rocks are called sedimentary because they were formed from sediments. In time, tiny droplets of oil seeped into layers of these porous rocks and were held there the way a sponge holds water.

Over millions of years the earth's crust was shifting. Old sea floors, and the oil they held, were in some cases changed to land areas. Others were pushed deeper into the sea. The earth shifted and continents changed in appearance.

This is why oil-bearing rock layers are today sometimes found far inland, and also why some of the most productive oil fields are located in desert regions. Millions of years ago they may have been areas under water.

WHY DOES A CACTUS HAVE SPINES?

The cactus is a remarkable example of how, if plants and animals are to survive, they must be fitted for the climates and places in which they live.

Cacti are plants that live in hot, dry regions, so going without water for long periods is a problem. As the climate became drier, the roots of cacti gradu-

ally spread out, closer to the surface of the ground. That's why cacti can absorb water quickly from the earth when there is a rainfall.

The water has to be stored. This is done in the spongy or hollow stem of a cactus plant. What's more, the outer layer of the plant is thick and waxy, to prevent the escape of water.

Other plants have leaves which give off water in sunlight. Cactus plants have spines—and these prevent the loss of water. But the spines help save the life of the cactus in another way, too. Suppose there are thirsty animals roaming about in search of water. There is water in the cactus plant—but can you imagine any animal taking a bite at a cactus?

Except for their special structures that enable them to store water, cacti are regular flowering plants with blossoms that develop into seed-bearing fruits. In fact, the flowers of most cacti are very beautiful. When a desert is in full bloom, you can see bright yellow, red, and purple blooms springing from the polished stems of the cacti.

True cacti are native only to the Western Hemisphere. They grow mainly in the dry lands of South America, Central America, and the southwestern United States.

WHAT IS AN EARTHQUAKE BELT?

Earthquakes are tremblings or vibrations of the earth's surface. The real cause of earthquakes is usually a "fault" in the rocks of the earth's crust—a break along which one rock mass has rubbed on another with very great force and friction.

Because of this, earthquakes do not occur in all parts of the world. They are confined to certain definite areas, which are called "belts." The most important belt is the rim of the Pacific Ocean, where most of the world's earthquakes have occurred.

This belt begins at the southern tip of Chile, reaches up the Pacific coast of South America to Central America (branching into the Caribbean), runs along the Mexican coast to California, and on to Alaska.

But that isn't the end of it. The belt continues from Alaska to Kamchatka. Passing through the Kurile Islands and the Aleutian Islands, it stretches on to Japan, the Philippines, Indonesia, New Guinea, and through various South Pacific islands.

Most of the big earthquakes in history have taken place within the Pacific belt. However, another earthquake belt branches off from Japan. It runs through China, India, Iran, Turkey, Greece, and the Mediterranean.

In some regions, such as Japan, earthquakes occur almost every day. Fortunately, most of these earthquakes are not severe and cause no damage. On the other hand, in the New England states there have been no destructive earthquakes since the last Ice Age, many thousands of years ago.

WHERE DOES MONEY FOR TAXES GO?

Taxation is the process by which governments get the money to pay for the things that the people want governments to do. In the United States, city and state governments and the national government collect taxes to pay for the many services which the people have decided the government should provide. It is much cheaper and more efficient to have schools and streets, fire and police departments, and the armed forces run by the government than to have each family try to provide its own education, highways, and protection.

The expenses of all kinds of governments have increased greatly over the years. The main reason for the increase in the cost of running the national government is national defense. In the states, cities, and towns the need for government spending has also increased.

It is necessary to have better streets and highways to take care of the large number of automobiles. More and better schools are needed, and larger universities are necessary. People want to have better hospitals, parks, and other facilities that may be provided by cities and towns.

The federal income tax is the most important source of funds for operation of the United States Government. Cities and towns get most of their money from property taxes. States get their money more and more from income taxes and sales taxes. Without these taxes, none of the services, help, and protection that people want would be possible.

WHAT IS INFLATION?

Basically, inflation is a rise in prices. Families, businesses, and government groups are all buyers. The things they buy are called goods and services. During an inflation people spend money faster than goods are being made. It is a period when too many dollars are chasing too few goods. During an inflation a dollar buys less.

Even if we knew all the causes of inflations, we might not be able to keep them from happening. Sometimes government spending is blamed for starting an inflation. Sometimes businesses and labor unions are blamed. Even family spending is blamed. Often inflations are caused by wars.

In an inflation, a steady rise in prices cuts back the amount that a dollar will buy. Then people hurry to buy before costs get any higher. Then businessmen think that there is a growing demand for their products. So they put money into new products, machinery, and factories.

This creates a greater demand for workers. People get bigger incomes and they spend their extra money. Businessmen see that their goods are selling well and borrow money to expand their businesses.

The people who suffer during an inflation are the savers, creditors (the people who have loaned money), people on pensions, and those who earn a fixed salary.

Before a government tries to control an inflation, it tries to understand what is causing it. If the wrong controls are used, they may not solve the problem.

WHY DON'T ALL COUNTRIES HAVE A COMMON FORM OF MONEY?

Money is not a metal coin or a piece of printed paper. It is not a nickel or dollar bill, a French franc, an Italian lira, a Spanish peseta, or a Russian ruble. Why? Because, while these things are used as money, so is a pile of stones on a certain Pacific island.

In other words, all of these things are only symbols. They represent something real. The simplest way to define money is to say that it is a convenient means of exchange and a measure of the value of goods and labor. When a person wants something, he can exchange his form of money for the desired object. He can also exchange his services for money.

Down through history, money has gone through many changes. Cattle was an early form of money. Grain and salt later came into use as money. In early societies around the world, different objects and products were used as money. Later on, coins came to be used, and then—about three hundred years ago— paper money came into general use.

As these more modern forms of money developed, local governments began to control the form of money and its value. Each country had its own form of money—and this is still true today. We simply haven't reached the stage of civilization in the world where all the people, wherever they live, use the same money.

WHAT IS A STOCK?

Stocks and bonds are certificates that business companies sell to the public to raise money. To start a new company, or to buy new equipment for an existing company, usually requires a very large amount of money. To raise the money, the company sells thousands, sometimes millions, of shares of stock.

When a person buys stock in a company, he becomes one of the company's owners. As an owner, a shareholder hopes to receive a dividend, or a share in the company's profits. The amount of the dividend may change from year to year, depending on the kind of business the company has done during the year.

There are two types of stock: common stock and preferred stock. The owner of the common stock has the right to attend the yearly stockholders' meeting and vote for the directors of the company.

Preferred stock is so named because its owners have certain rights that owners of common stock do not have. When dividends are paid, first preference goes to the holders of preferred stocks. The dividends paid on preferred stocks have a set rate, while dividends on common stocks depend on how well the company is doing. If the company goes out of business, holders of preferred stock are paid off before the holders of common stock.

When a person buys stocks or bonds, he buys from another investor. When he sells, he sells to another investor. The marketplace for this selling and buying of stocks is the Stock Exchange.

Stocks are bought and sold through a broker. His business is to buy and sell stocks for investors. The price of stocks may go up or down for a variety of reasons relating to the company concerned, business conditions in general, and so on.

WHAT IS ECOLOGY?

Every living thing has its own way of life. The way of life depends partly on its own form and activities and partly on its environment (surroundings). Every organism (living thing) is affected by all that surrounds it—whether living or nonliving. And in turn each organism has some effect on its surroundings. Each organism is part of a complex web of life.

At the same time, every organism lives as part of a community, or group, of other organisms. These organisms, too, make up part of the surroundings.

Therefore, when we study an animal or plant in its natural surroundings, we are really studying a web of life. A scientist who studies these webs of life is called an ecologist. His subject is ecology, which comes from two Greek words meaning "study of the home, or surroundings."

Ecology studies the relations of living things to the world in which they live and tells us, among other things, how we can most effectively use and conserve our resources. It deals with such things as: How can we make the best use of our land? How can we save our soil, our forests, our wild life? How can we reduce the great losses caused by harmful insects? These are examples of the practical questions the ecologist asks and tries to answer.

HOW WERE THE GREAT LAKES FORMED?

The five Great Lakes together form the greatest connected area of fresh water on earth. In fact, one of them, Lake Superior, is bigger than any other fresh-water lake in the world. The only saltwater lake that is bigger is the Caspian Sea.

The basins of the Great Lakes were probably scooped out by glaciers during the Ice Age. As the glaciers pushed down from the north, the great moving weight of the ice made these valleys deeper and wider.

Then, when the ice melted, it left huge beds of sand, gravel, and rock where the rim of the glaciers had been. These beds blocked what used to be the outlets of the valleys.

THE GREAT LAKES

At the same time, as the weight of the ice was removed, the land began to rise, beginning in the southwest. This caused the surface of the region to be tilted, so that water flowed from the southwest to northeast. By the time the ice had retreated, all the lakes were draining down this tilt into the St. Lawrence River and the Atlantic Ocean.

What keeps the Great Lakes filled with fresh water? Some streams do drain into them, but most of the rivers in the area flow away from the Great Lakes basin. The main source of supply for the lakes is the ground water that lies close to the surface of this whole region.

The lake beds are like basins that dip below the level of this ground water, and so they are kept filled by seepage and by the flow of many small springs. So the Great Lakes are really like huge drainage ponds or rain pools—and in this way have a constant supply of fresh water.

The combined area of the Great Lakes and their channels is 94.710 square miles.

WHAT IS OLIVE OIL?

The ancient Greeks had a legend that the olive tree was a gift to them from the goddess Athena, which was why they named the city of Athens after her. The boundaries of estates in Greece were marked by olive trees. The tree was to ancient Greeks a symbol of freedom, hope, mercy, prayer, purity, and order. A crown of olive leaves was the reward given to winners at the Olympic games in ancient Greece.

Olive oil has been obtained from the olive and used for many purposes since very ancient times. Before soap was discovered, wealthy Greeks and Romans had the custom of anointing the body with olive oil. In the Mediterranean countries it has been used as we use butter and other fats for cooking.

In ancient times the oil was extracted from olives by crushing the fruit with large stone rollers. After crushing, the mashed olives were put between cloth mats and squeezed.

Today the process has been refined and mechanized. Modern grinders crush the olives. Hydraulic presses squeeze out the oil. The oil is then carefully filtered to clarify it, that is, make it clear and pure. The oil is about 15 to 30 per cent of the total weight of a fresh, ripe olive.

WHAT IS THE HIGHEST MOUNTAIN IN THE WORLD?

First, what is a mountain? A mountain is a part of the earth's surface that stands high above its surroundings. Mountains differ greatly in size and ruggedness. Some are huge, steep masses several miles high. Others are low and gentle. A mountain rises at least 1,000 feet above the surrounding land.

Some mountains are isolated peaks. But more often they are grouped together in a mountain range. Some mountain ranges have hundreds or even thousands of peaks.

Mountains rise not only from land areas but also from the bottom of the sea. In fact, the deep ocean basins hold some of the mightiest mountains on earth. If we would consider the total height of a mountain to include what is below the sea and what is above the sea, the tallest mountain of all would be Mauna Kea on the island of Hawaii. It is 13,796 feet above sea level and 16,000 feet or so below the sea. So its total height of about 30,000 to 32,000 feet would make it the tallest in the world.

The highest mountain above ground is Mount Everest, on the Nepal-China border. It is 29,028 feet high. The second highest is K2 or Mount Godwin Austen in Kashmir. It is 28,250 feet high.

The highest mountain in North America is McKinley, 20,320 feet. The highest in Europe is Mount Elbrus, in the Soviet Union. It is 18,481 feet high. The highest in Africa is Kilimanjaro, 19,565 feet. The highest mountain in South America is Aconcagua, on the Argentine-Chile border, 22,835 feet high. The highest in Australia is Kosciusko, which is only 7,305 feet high.

WHY IS IT COOLER ON TOP OF A MOUNTAIN?

Our atmosphere is divided into layers, each different from the others. The main layers are called the troposphere, the stratosphere, and the ionosphere. Together, they form a blanket several hundred miles thick.

The troposphere is the bottom layer of the atmosphere. This is where we live. Above the United States and southern Canada, the troposphere is about 40,000 feet (nearly eight miles) thick.

Instruments carried aloft in balloons have proved that the temperature drops steadily in the troposphere. The higher one goes into the troposphere the lower the temperature becomes. For each one thousand feet, the temperature drops about 3.5 degrees Fahrenheit.

So when we go up a mountain to the top, we are going up into the troposphere. A mountain that is about a mile high can thus be about 15 degrees cooler in temperature at the top. And there are mountain peaks that are more than five miles (more than 26,000 feet) high! No wonder it's always cold up there. At the top of the troposphere, the temperature is nearly 70 degrees below zero.

The air is always warmest near the earth's surface. The reason is that the sun heats the earth and the earth gives off heat that warms the air. The sun does not warm the atmosphere directly.

WHY DID INDIANS TAKE SCALPS?

Most of us think that only the Indians took scalps, and that the white man would have nothing to do with this practice. But there are some interesting facts concerning scalping.

Scalping means partly cutting and partly tearing off the skin of the head, with the hair attached. The victim could be living or dead. Scalping goes back to very ancient times. It was done by savage and barbarous peoples of Asia and Europe long before it was done by the American Indians.

And among the Indians it was not done by many tribes. For example, the Indians in the Canadian Northwest and along the whole Pacific Coast never practiced scalping.

A scalp was regarded, by those who did this, as a trophy of victory. It was a sign that the scalper had courage and skill in fighting. Among some tribes the scalps were used in religious ceremonies.

When the American colonies were fighting the Indians, many of the colonies offered rewards of money for Indian scalps. In 1724, Massachusetts offered about $500 for each Indian scalp. In 1755, the same colony offered about $200 for the scalps of male Indians over 12 years of age, and about $100 for the scalps of women and children. So this is something in our history not to be proud of.

HAS THE ICE AGE REALLY ENDED?

Ice ages are times when thick sheets of ice have spread over large parts of the continents. The ice sheets form when glaciers of high mountains and polar regions grow to great size.

There have been several ice ages. The last one, often called the Ice Age, began about 2,500,000 years ago. Four times during the Ice Age great sheets of ice advanced over the land and four times they melted and drew back. The last advance ended about 18,000 years ago. About 6,000 years ago the continents of the Northern Hemisphere were once more almost free of ice.

But Antarctica and Greenland did not lose their ice. They are still covered by ice sheets between one and two miles thick. This raises the question: Has the Ice Age really ended, or will glaciers advance again?

Scientists don't have the answer, because it really depends on what causes ice ages. And this is one of the great mysteries of science. There are many theories about what makes the earth's climate become colder and warmer. One is that there are actual changes in the amount of energy given off by the sun from time to time. Another is that dust from volcanic eruptions could cut off large amounts of sunlight from the earth.

Another theory is that changes in the amount of carbon dioxide in the air would cause great climate changes. Or climate changes could be related to changes in the distance between the earth and the sun and in the tilt of the earth's axis. And there are still other theories. So until we know exactly what causes sheets of ice to advance over the land and then melt and draw back, we won't know whether the last Ice Age has really ended.

WHAT IS A FOLK SONG?

Since the beginning of the human race, people have been singing folk songs. There are so many different kinds of folk songs that it is hard to define a folk song. Basically, folk songs tell us how people feel about life.

One type is work songs, sung by workers on plantations and the railroads, songs for building roads, and so on. There are songs about occupations, which are sung at any time. They may be about shepherds, shoemakers, blacksmiths, tailors. They can be about mills and mines—and about cowboys.

Another type of folk song has to do with love and marriage. Songs such as "I know where I'm going," and "Frankie and Johnny," and "Matilda," are examples of this type. Children's songs and games can also be folk songs.

Some folk songs combine fact and fancy and are sung just for fun. They might be nonsense songs or tall tales. A type of folk song—the play-party song

—developed from children's games, such as "London Bridge" and "All Around the Mulberry Bush." There are also folk songs that have to do with animals.

Still another type is the religious folk song. The "spiritual" is one of the most beautiful of this kind. There are also folk songs that have to do with the seasons.

And there are still more: wedding songs, lullabies, songs of mourning, songs of war and military life.

DO ANY CANNIBALS EXIST TODAY?

It is possible that the earliest humans fed on human flesh, as on any other. There is some evidence that cannibalism existed in central Europe in the late ice age, and possibly among the most ancient Egyptians.

At one time cannibalism was customary in most of Polynesia, in New Zealand, and in Fiji. It also occurred in Australia and New Guinea. Most of equatorial Africa had cannibalism at one time. It was also widespread in northern South America and the West Indies.

But cannibalism was seldom practiced only to obtain food. It had to do with warfare, or with the idea that one could acquire the enemy's strength by eating him, or that certain magical things happened when this was done.

As civilization spread throughout the world, cannibalism ended or was prohibited by police and government. During the last few hundred years it has existed only in certain tropical and subtropical areas.

It is probable that cannibalism today occurs only in the most remote districts of New Guinea, perhaps in the northeast Congo, and in certain inaccessible parts of South America.

DID THE VIKINGS VISIT NORTH AMERICA?

The homeland of the Vikings was Denmark, Norway, and Sweden. Starting in A.D. 787, for about 250 years, they explored, discovered, and plundered countries all over Europe. They built cities in Ireland, penetrated all of England, gained a province in France, raided Spain, Italy, and North Africa, established a kingdom in Russia, settled Iceland, and founded a colony in Greenland.

Did they also discover America? There is now evidence that they did. About the year 1000 Leif Ericson sailed west from Greenland with 35 men. They made two landfalls, and finally reached a pleasant place where game, grass, and salmon abounded. They called this Vinland (Wineland).

The site of Vinland was long sought and never found by modern explorers. Many scholars refused to take seriously the old Scandinavian sagas that told of Viking expeditions to the New World—because there was nothing to confirm them. There were no ruins, no buried arms, no stones with inscriptions.

Then, in 1963, a Norwegian explorer, Dr. Helge Ingstad, unearthed on the tip of Newfoundland the remains of nine buildings and a smithy, which were unquestionably Viking in origin.

By modern methods these relics can be dated at about the year 1000, almost five hundred years before the voyage of Columbus. They may have been Leif Ericson's Vinland or they may have been built by other Viking voyagers to the New World. But they are proof that the Vikings did visit America.

WHAT ARE ABORIGINES?

The earliest known inhabitants of a region are the aborigines. They are the people who were there before any new settlers arrived from another part of the world.

The word comes from the Latin *aborigine*, meaning "from the beginning." It was first used by Roman writers to describe the tribes who originally lived in the territory on which Rome developed.

Bushmen are described as the aborigines of South Africa because they occupied the land before Bantu-speaking Negro tribes. The primitive tribal people who occupied Australia before the coming of the Europeans are called the Australian aborigines.

They are probably the best-known aborigines in the world today. The Australian aborigines live mainly inland and in the remote northern coastal areas. They total about 50,000 people. Their ancestors led a nomadic life and wandered about in tribes. Today, fewer than a third of these aborigines live that way.

The Australian aborigines belong to a separate family of man, and are known as Australoids. It is not known how long they have been in Australia. Before they were influenced by the Europeans, they wore no clothes, built no permanent dwellings, cultivated no crops, and lived as nomadic hunters.

Now many of them have organized together to fight for their rights in Australia. They have the right to vote at federal elections and are entitled to all the social benefits available to other Australians.

WHAT IS WITCHCRAFT?

At one time a great many people believed in witches and in witchcraft. A witch was a person of great power and authority, whose goal was to do harm, and who worked with the help of the devil. The mischief that such a person was able to commit was witchcraft.

Witchcraft could be directed against a personal enemy, or even against a community. Even hurricanes and epidemics were thought to be the result of witchcraft. Because people then lived in fear, ignorance, and superstition, witchcraft was an easy way of explaining unforeseen disasters.

Early societies and religions forbade witchcraft on pain of death. The Old Testament says: "Thou shalt not suffer a witch to live." In later times, the Christian churches fought against witchcraft. In 1484, the Pope issued a papal bull formally condemning witchcraft.

Witch hunts took place in the American colonies. Between 1647 and 1663 hundreds of people in Massachusetts and Connecticut were accused of witchcraft, and 14 were hanged. But with the beginning of the 18th century, belief in witches faded. For the first time people began to understand the real causes of the things they had feared—drought, thunder and lightning, mental and physical illness.

WHERE DO METALS COME FROM?

Pure metals are chemical elements. This means that they cannot be broken down into other substances. There are over a hundred chemical elements known, and about 80 of these are metals.

A few metals, such as gold, platinum, silver, and sometimes copper, are found in the earth in their pure state. Most metals, however, are not found free in nature. They are found only in chemical combinations with other elements.

Chemical compounds that are found in nature are called minerals. Minerals that are valuable for the metals they contain are called ores.

The value of an ore depends on how much metal is in the ore and how costly it is to remove the metal from the ore. It also depends on the demand for the metal.

Many processes are used to obtain pure metal from ore. Some ores need to go through only a few steps, while other ores must go through many steps.

When ore comes from the mine, it usually contains large amounts of unwanted material, such as clay and stone. This worthless material is usually removed before the valuable part of the ore is processed further.

Copper and gold were probably the first metals man learned to use. They occur in nature in a free state as well as in ores. Copper was used as long ago as 5000 B.C. Gold was first used some time before 4000 B.C.

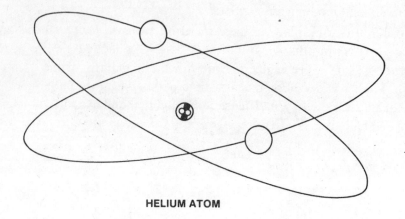

HELIUM ATOM

WHO DISCOVERED ATOMS?

The idea of the atom as the smallest possible particle of any substance goes back to the ancient Greeks. Today we know the atom is not the smallest particle—there are other particles within the atom itself. And we also know that we still don't know a great deal about the atom.

The first man to develop a scientific atomic theory was John Dalton, an English chemist who lived at the beginning of the 19th century. He found that gases, as well as solids and liquids, were made up of unbelievably tiny particles which he (like the ancient Greeks) called atoms. He figured out relative weights for the atoms of those elements with which he was familiar.

At the end of the 19th century, Ernest Rutherford developed the idea of a "solar-system" atom. In an atom there was supposed to be a center, a heavy nucleus carrying a positive charge of electricity, which was surrounded by negatively charged electrons. The electrons traveled around the nucleus like planets around the sun.

Later on, Niels Bohr developed a new theory about the atom. He showed that the electrons could revolve only in certain orbits or energy levels. When electrons moved from one level to another they gave off energy.

But what man knows about the structure of the atom is constantly changing as new experiments give us new information.

WHAT IS THE OZONE LAYER?

Man is becoming more and more aware that things he does in his daily life can have an effect on the climate, the water and food he takes in, the air he breathes, and so on. There is now some concern that things we release into the air can have a harmful effect on "the ozone layer."

What is the ozone layer and why is it important? The earth is surrounded by a thick blanket of air, the "atmosphere." Earth's atmosphere is one of the things that make it a planet of life. It is the air we breathe. It shields us from certain dangerous rays sent out by the sun. It protects the earth from extremes of heat and cold. And it serves us in many other ways.

Our atmosphere is divided into layers, each different from the others. The bottom layer, about ten miles high, is the troposphere. Most of our weather takes shape in the troposphere. The second layer of air, going from a height of ten miles to a height of 30 miles, is the stratosphere.

Somewhere between 12 and 22 miles up, in the middle of the stratosphere, is the "ozone layer." It is a layer of ozone, which is a form of oxygen. Here the winds have died away and the air is warm. It is the ozone that makes the air warm.

This gas absorbs most of the ultraviolet rays sent out by the sun. One result is the band of warm air. But more importantly, the ozone stops most of the ultraviolet rays from reaching the earth. A few of them are good for us, but a large dose would actually broil us alive. So you can see why it is important not to let anything we send into the air have an effect on the ozone layer.

CHAPTER 3
THE HUMAN BODY

WHAT CAUSES AN EARACHE?

There are many different conditions that cause an earache, and even the form of the earache varies a great deal. Aside from mechanical injuries, most earaches arise from some type of bacterial infection.

In many cases an earache is caused by a foreign body that has become trapped in the ear. Children sometimes deliberately put something into their ear or another child's ear.

Sometimes earache is caused by hardened wax in the ear. This, and the removal of any object in the ear, should be done by a physician, because he knows how to avoid injury to the delicate parts of the ear.

Infection of the outer ear may be the result of using unclean hairpins, matches, or other objects to relieve itching of the ear caused by wax. These objects may break the skin and introduce infection. This causes a boil to form, the ear swells up, and there will be painful earaches.

A fungus infection of the outer ear and canal can produce a swelling of the canal which causes pain. Sometimes shooting pains are felt in the ear after a cold or other respiratory infection. The eardrum, which divides the outer ear from the middle ear, may become inflamed.

The middle ear may become infected simply because the person has blown the nose incorrectly. Both nostrils should be blown at the same time, because blowing only one side at a time may force infectious material into the sinuses. And there are many other causes of earaches, too. So it is advisable to see a doctor when one has frequent earaches.

WHAT IS YELLOW FEVER?

Did you know that when the French tried to build a Panama canal, they had to give up chiefly because the construction crews were struck down by yellow fever?

In 1900, Walter Reed discovered the cause of yellow fever and how it was transmitted. As a result, work on the canal was able to be done and the canal was completed in 1914.

Yellow fever is an acute disease in which the patient has fever, jaundice, and vomiting. If it is an isolated case, the attack may be mild and the patient is fairly certain to recover. But if there is an epidemic of yellow fever, as many as 50 per cent of the patients may die.

Yellow fever is caused by a virus which attacks the liver chiefly. The liver cells are extensively damaged, which results in jaundice. In fact, it is the yellow-to-brown color of the skin which gives the disease its name.

The virus is transmitted by mosquitoes. The female mosquito of a certain species sucks the blood of a person with yellow fever during the first three days after that person became infected. After about twelve days, the virus in the mosquito becomes infective. Then, when it bites a person who is not immune to yellow fever, that person will develop the disease.

There is no drug that can cure yellow fever, so prevention is what is important. There is a vaccine that makes people immune to yellow fever. Also, once a person has it, he is immune. And, of course, mosquito control in those areas where yellow fever is found is also a way to prevent it.

WHY IS THERE STILL NO CURE FOR CANCER?

First, what is cancer? Basically, it is when the process of cell division in the body gets out of hand. As the new "wild" cells continue to divide, they form a larger and larger mass of tissue. So cancer is an uncontrolled growth (and spread) of body cells.

Cancer can occur in any kind of cell. Since there are many different kinds of cells, there are many different kinds of cancer. In man alone there are hundreds of different kinds of cancer—so cancer is not one disease but a large family of diseases. This is one of the problems in finding a cure for cancer.

One approach in dealing with the problem of cancer is to learn what agents cause cancer. Scientists also need to know exactly how such agents cause normal cells to produce cancerous cells. In this way they hope to be able to prevent the disease. Other lines of research involve the search for agents to destroy the cancer cells in the body, just as modern antibiotics destroy bacterial cells.

Scientists have found many cancer-causing agents that are chemicals. Steps have been taken by governments to keep such chemicals out of food and to prevent other forms of contact with them. Such actions do help prevent cancer.

Because of the close links between cancer and viruses in certain animals, more and more scientists are coming to believe that many types of cancer are caused by viruses. But exactly how a virus can produce cancer in the human body is still not known.

So the search for the causes of cancer is a difficult one, but much progress is being made. Eventually, it may be discovered that the different kinds of cancer have little in common. Or it may be that all the different agents work in the same way. But at present we still don't know.

WHAT IS CEREBRAL PALSY?

Cerebral palsy is a condition in which the patient has little or no control over the movements of his muscles. It happens when one of the three main areas of the brain that control muscular activity is damaged.

One such area of the brain is called the motor cortex. This is where all movements that are planned and controllable start. When it is damaged, there is stiffness of the muscles.

A group of nerve cells in the brain, called basal ganglia, hold back or restrain certain types of muscle activity. When there is damage in this area, unplanned movements of the muscles occur. It might be slow, squirming, and twisting movements of the arms. Or it may be slight shaking or violent jerking.

The third area of the brain, called the cerebellar area, controls muscle coordination and balance. If this area is injured, there is a lack of balance and clumsiness.

There are many causes of cerebral palsy. The brain may not develop as it should before birth. The mother may be sick or injured during pregnancy. The brain may be injured during birth. Difficulty in breathing at the time of birth may prevent oxygen from getting into the blood and injure nerve cells.

Treatment is a long, slow, and continuous process. The aim of it, which must be realized, is not to restore the child to a normal condition. It is to make the child useful to himself and the world, so that he will be happier. Muscle training is the most valuable way of treating children with cerebral palsy.

HOW DOES THE BRAIN SEND MESSAGES TO THE BODY?

The brain can get signals, add them up, and signal back for action in a split second. Different parts of the brain do different things.

The medulla, at the top of the spinal cord, controls nerves that are in charge of certain muscles and glands. The medulla keeps your heart beating, your lungs taking in air, and your stomach digesting food.

The cerebellum controls body movement and balance. The cerebrum is where thinking, learning, remembering, deciding, and awareness take place. The sensations of seeing, hearing, smelling, tasting, and touching are centered here. So are body feelings.

Scientists still do not understand how the brain does its work. But they have learned that the messages that travel through the nervous system—to and from the brain—are weak electrical charges.

Nerves are made up of nerve cells. A nerve cell consists of a central cell body with a number of threadlike parts reaching out from it. Messages are passed from cell to cell through these threads.

The billions of nerve cells in the body form a huge network that leads toward the spine. Along the way nerves from different parts of the body come together in thick bundles. A thick cable of nerves runs up the hollow of the spine to the brain. One set of nerves in the cable carries messages from the senses to the brain. Another set carries messages from the brain to the muscles and glands. The brain sorts out the signals and makes the right connections.

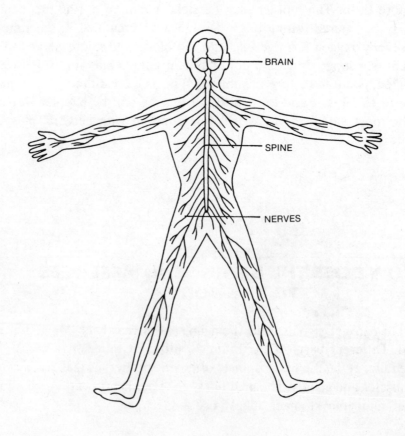

WHY DO WE NEED OXYGEN?

Animals can go for weeks without food, and for days without water. But without oxygen they die in a few minutes.

Oxygen is a chemical element. It is the most abundant element on earth and it is all around you. It makes up about one-fifth of the air (most of the rest of the air is nitrogen).

Oxygen combines with almost all other elements. In living creatures, oxygen is combined with hydrogen, carbon, and other substances. In a human being it accounts for two-thirds of body weight.

At normal temperatures oxygen combines with other elements very slowly. When oxygen combines with other elements, new substances, called oxides, are formed. The combining process is called oxidation.

Oxidation goes on all the time in living creatures. Food is the fuel of living cells. As food is oxidized, energy is released. This energy is used for moving the body and for building new body substances. The slow oxidation in living creatures is often called internal respiration.

In man, oxygen is breathed in through the lungs. From the lungs, oxygen passes into the bloodstream and is carried to all parts of the body. The breathing process supplies the cells with oxygen for respiration. So we need oxygen for the energy to keep the body functioning.

People who have trouble breathing are often placed in oxygen tents. Here the patient breathes in air that is from 40 to 60 percent oxygen. The patient thus uses little energy to get the oxygen he needs.

While oxygen is continually being removed from the air, the supply of oxygen never seems to get used up. Plants give off oxygen as they make food, and this helps keep up the supply of oxygen.

WHAT IS ENDOCRINOLOGY?

Certain organs in the body produce chemical substances that keep the body in proper working order. These chemical substances are called hormones. The group of organs that produce hormones is called the endocrine system. And the study of these organs and hormones is called endocrinology.

The organs of the endocrine system are called "glands of internal secretion" because they send their substances directly into the bloodstream to be distributed throughout the body.

The endocrine glands are: the pituitary, the thyroid, the parathyroids, the adrenals, the testes, the ovaries, part of the pancreas, and the thymus. Some of these produce many hormones and others produce only one.

The endocrine system is responsible for regulating many functions of the body. For example, the rate of growth and final size of the body, the body contour, the distribution of hair, total weight, and the masculine or feminine aspect of the body are all influenced by hormones.

They also regulate the amount of urine produced, the body temperature, the rate of metabolism, the calcium and sugar levels in the blood, the transformation of proteins into energy-giving substances. How they are able to do all this is still not fully understood by experts on the subject.

The reproductive system is especially affected by hormones. And they are also a great factor in the personality of the individual. A person's mental and physical alertness, and masculinity or femininity, are influenced by hormones.

WHAT IS HEMOGLOBIN?

Most of the cells in the blood are red corpuscles. Millions and millions of red cells circulate in the bloodstream.

The red corpuscles contain a protein called hemoglobin. Hemoglobin is a pigment (coloring matter) containing iron. Our blood is red in color because of the combination of hemoglobin and oxygen.

But hemoglobin has a more important function than just giving the blood its color. It has the ability to combine loosely with oxygen. It is this ability that makes it possible for the red corpuscles to deliver oxygen to the cells of the body.

Oxygen is part of the air breathed into the lungs. The red corpuscles in the bloodstream pass through the lungs, where the hemoglobin picks up oxygen. The red corpuscles, traveling through the bloodstream, release oxygen to the body's cells.

When the oxygen is released, hemoglobin takes up carbon dioxide from the cells. This gas is waste that is formed when the cells burn food. The red blood corpuscles, loaded with carbon dioxide, return to the lungs.

Here an exchange takes place. Carbon dioxide is dropped (to be breathed out) and fresh oxygen is picked up. Then the red corpuscles continue on their way, carrying oxygen to cells throughout the body.

This is why foods containing iron are important to our health. Iron stimulates the production of red blood cells and increases the amount of hemoglobin in those cells.

HOW DO WE SWALLOW?

The act of swallowing food is quite a complicated process. It is done by nerves, muscles, ligaments and glands. Included in the process are the larynx, the uvula, the epiglottis, the soft palate, the tongue, lips, nose, lungs, diaphragm, the abdominal muscles, and the brain!

First our teeth cut and grind the food, which is moistened by saliva. The tongue kneads the food into a bolus (a large pill). In the act of swallowing, the soft palate in the back of the mouth is raised so that food won't enter the nose.

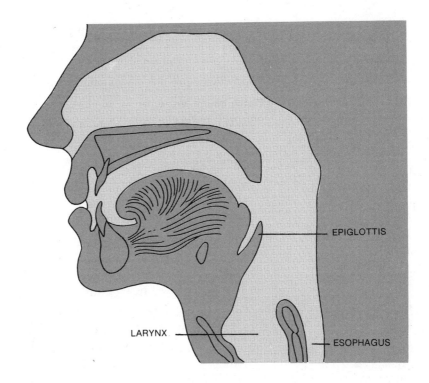

Then the food enters the pharynx. Here the windpipe is open on top. To prevent food from entering the windpipe, the epiglottis, which is at the root of the tongue, comes down to cover the entrance to the windpipe. The bolus then passes into the gullet, or esophagus, which is about ten inches long.

The walls of the gullet consist of muscle fibers, and the food is pushed through the gullet by the contractions of its walls. Liquids pass quickly down the esophagus; a bolus of food takes about eight seconds to go through. So swallowing of food is not a matter of having it fall down into the stomach. It requires muscular action. That's why it's actually possible to eat and drink while hanging with one's head downward.

What makes the muscles contract during swallowing? In the wall of the alimentary canal are nerves which react to the presence of food. The food touches the wall of the canal, stimulates the nerves, and the nerves cause the muscles to contract—pushing the food through.

WHY DO WE SMOKE?

Millions and millions of people know that smoking is believed to be harmful and even dangerous to the health, yet millions and millions continue smoking—or even start smoking. Why?

Experts in various fields say that the beginning of smoking, and the process by which it becomes a habit, are complex and not fully understood. Of course, certain things can be pointed out, as those that get people started on smoking, and others that keep them at it—but the point is that it isn't just a simple matter.

For example, we know that most people start smoking because other people around them do it. Do you know that in the 12th grade, from 40 to 55 percent of children are smokers? By the age of 25, about 60 percent of men and 36 percent of women are smokers. Children feel it makes them seem "adult" to smoke, and other children urge them to smoke, and they see their parents smoking—so they start smoking, too.

The effect that smoking has on a person then acts to strengthen the habit. For example, nicotine has an effect on the heart and the nervous system. Smoking one or two cigarettes causes an increase in the heart rate and a slight rise in blood pressure. The effect on the nervous system is chiefly tranquilizing and relaxing. People want these effects, or feel they need them, or come to depend on having them at certain times and in certain situations—and so they go on smoking.

WHAT ARE PHAGOCYTES?

In the body there are millions of lymph nodes, which are balls of cells surrounded by connective tissue and muscle fibers. The cells that come from the lymph organs are called lymph cells.

But they also have several other names. They are called white blood cells. They are called leukocytes, because they float in the blood as colorless bodies alongside the red blood cells. They are called wander cells, because they wander about through the body.

And they are called phagocytes, which means "scavenger" cells, because they have the ability to ingest foreign bodies. There are about a thousand times as many red blood cells as white cells.

The number of white cells in the blood increases during digestion, after strenuous exercise, during fever, and in the course of various infectious diseases. This is why every complete medical examination includes making a white blood cell count.

The white blood cells, or phagocytes, can be compared to policemen, soldiers, street cleaners, firemen, and first-aid men of the blood. Whenever there is a foreign substance in the body, a dying cell, or some vital activity is disturbed, they go into action.

For example, if a splinter penetrates the skin, it is attacked by a whole army of these cells. They gnaw at it. They secrete digestive substances around it and try to dissolve it. They eat into the tissue around the splinter so it will become liquefied.

This liquefied tissue is called pus. If we have a wound that gives off pus, it is a sign that there is something there which the body wants to remove. A large collection of pus is called an abscess.

WHY DO WE NEED SO MUCH SLEEP?

If we think of the human body as a "machine," it has one big weakness compared to other machines. They can work around the clock. The human machine must have a chance, at regular intervals, to restore tired organs and tissues of the body, to do repair work, and to get rid of wastes that have accumulated during the day. This is done during sleep.

When the body is asleep, everything slows down. The rate of metabolism is at its lowest. The blood pressure drops. The pulse rate is slower. Breathing is slowed down. Even the temperature drops a little.

So the body needs sleep just to "keep going." But how much sleep does a person need? The surprising thing is that it varies with the individual. Of course, babies need more sleep than grownups. But as one grows older, less sleep is required. The one thing that matters is that we should have enough sleep so that when we wake up we are rested and refreshed.

There are some people who say that four hours of sleep a night is all they need, but this is not enough for most people. There are some who are "long sleepers" and seem to need ten or more hours. The great German philospher Kant needed so much sleep that he had his servant wake him up after seven hours and force him to get out of bed—or he would sleep on and on!

By the way, a short sleep—which may last only 15 minutes or a half hour—may be more restful than a long sleep. This is because it is a deep sleep, when our body really relaxes and goes to sleep.

WHAT CHANGES THE RATE OF A HEARTBEAT?

Each beat of the human heart lasts about 0.8 seconds. The heart beats about 100,000 times a day. It also rests an equal number of times between beats. In one year, the heart beats about 40,000,000 times.

The beating of the heart is really a wave of contraction that takes place in the heart to send blood circulating through the body. So the rate of the heartbeat (or pulse rate) depends on the body's need of blood.

Change in the heartbeat is most often caused by work. Here is how this happens. When a muscle begins to function somewhere in the body, it produces carbonic acid. The molecules of carbonic acid are carried by the blood to a certain part of the heart, the right atrium, within ten seconds.

There are cells there that react to the presence of the carbonic acid molecules. And the reaction adjusts the rate of the heartbeat to the carbonic acid content of the blood. If the muscle stops working, and the carbonic acid content of the blood becomes lower, the action of the heart becomes slower.

But the action of the heart is related to the needs of the body as a whole. Mental excitement stimulates a nerve which makes the heart beat faster. When we are depressed or frightened, a different nerve is stimulated, which makes the heart beat slower.

The ordinary person cannot change the rate of his heartbeat by just wanting to do it. But there have been certain people who had this ability. There is the case of one man who was able to make his heart "stand still" so that people thought he was dead—and then was able to make it beat again.

WHY DO ALCOHOLIC BEVERAGES MAKE YOU DRUNK?

Alcohol is a narcotic, which is how we describe a substance which enters the nerve cells quickly and tends to paralyze them. But before any narcotic paralyzes, it stimulates nerve cells, putting them in a state of excitement. So alcohol first acts as a stimulant.

How does alcohol affect the brain? The first effect is a feeling of stimulation. Action and speech seem to be speeded up. The skin gets redder, blood pressure rises, the heart beats faster, and breathing is quickened.

But alcohol soon exerts a depressing effect on the brain. Our ability to observe, think, and pay attention is affected. As the higher functions of the brain are paralyzed, the power to control moods is lost.

Another serious effect is that inhibitions are relaxed. In our body nerve fibers called inhibitory fibers act as brakes in the nervous system. They are developed as the result of education and training, and make us disciplined, restrained people.

Under the influence of alcohol, these inhibitory fibers are paralyzed. Our controls become relaxed, our judgment is unclear, and we are ready to say and do things that we would never do if our minds were normal. Alcohol has produced a state of drunkenness!

Since alcohol does first act as a stimulant, if it is taken into the body in weak solutions, it will continue to act as a stimulant rather than as a narcotic.

WHAT CAUSES GOUT?

Gout is a disease that has been known since ancient times. At one time it was thought of as a "rich man's disease." This was because it was believed that gout was caused by eating too much and drinking too much wine—and, of course, this couldn't be done by poor people.

Gout is a condition of having too much uric acid in the blood. A person who has gout is unable to metabolize, or break down, certain proteins taken into the body. These proteins are called "purines" and are obtained from the diet of the person.

Among the foods with a high purine content are: sweetbreads, liver, kidney, sardines, anchovies, turkey, pork, beef, and many others. So a person with gout is usually advised by his doctor to avoid such foods.

Gout is a very painful disease, and the pain seems to come very suddenly. In 70 per cent of the cases, the first attack is in the large toe, and in 90 per cent of the cases the large toe is involved eventually.

Within hours, the joint swells, becomes hot, red, and tender. It hurts so much that a person with gout is very much afraid of being touched on the painful part. This feeling is typical of a patient with gout.

The acute condition lasts a few days or weeks, and then disappears completely—until the next attack. A person who is subject to attacks of gout may have them brought on not only by his diet, but by such things as physical strain, overwork, emotional strain, and allergy.

WHAT GIVES FOOD ITS TASTE?

The whole process of tasting is actually quite a complicated thing. First, we start with the taste buds, tiny wart-like bumps on the tongue called "papillae." An individual has about three thousand taste buds.

We taste when the molecules in a fluid strike the hairs in the taste buds and produce a reaction. Only substances in solution, where the atoms move about freely, can be tasted. A glass ball, for example, has no taste.

Anything that makes atoms move faster intensifies taste. Heat does this, and that's why hot coffee has a more bitter taste than cold coffee, why salt pork is saltier when it is warm, and why meat tastes better when it is hot.

Our taste buds register three or four different sensations: sweet, salt, bitter, and perhaps also sour. Different parts of the tongue are more sensitive to different tastes. The back of it is more sensitive to bitter, the sides to sour and salt, the tip to sweet.

Since almost all our foods are composed of various substances, they produce mixed sensations of taste. An apple is sour and sweet. And the taste sensation itself is a mixed sensation. There is no pure taste. We experience pressure, cold, heat, odor impressions as we taste. The combination of many sensations results in what we call the taste of food. And at least half of what we think of as "taste" is really odor! Coffee, tea, tobacco, apples, oranges, lemons, and other things really stimulate the sense of smell, as we enjoy them more than the sense of taste.

HOW FAST DOES OUR BLOOD FLOW?

Blood doesn't flow through the human body the way water flows through a regular series of pipes. The vessels through which blood is pumped out of the heart to all parts of the body are the arteries. But the arteries that are some distance from the heart keep on dividing and dividing until they become tiny vessels called capillaries. And the blood flows much more slowly through these vessels than it does through arteries.

Capillaries are fifty times thinner than a human hair, so that the blood corpuscles pass through them in single file. It takes a quantity of blood about one second to flow through a capillary.

Blood is constantly flowing through the heart. It takes about 1.5 seconds for a given quantity of blood to pass through the heart. Blood flows from the heart to the lung and back to the heart. This takes about 5 to 7 seconds.

Blood flows from the heart to the brain and back to the heart. This takes about eight seconds. The longest trip the blood has to make is from the heart through the trunk and the legs to the toes and then back to the heart. This takes about 18 seconds.

The time required for the blood to circulate through the entire body—that is, from the heart to the lung to the heart to the body to the heart—is about 23 seconds.

But the condition of the body has an effect on how fast the blood flows. For example, fever or work can increase the number of heartbeats and make the blood flow twice as fast. A single blood cell makes about three thousand round trips through the body's circulation in one day.

WHAT VITAMINS DO WE NEED?

The answer is simple: we need them all. When we don't get a particular vitamin, the conditions that result are known as deficiency diseases.

Vitamins are very different from each other in structure. But each vitamin is a substance that the body cannot manufacture, but must have. So a vitamin is essential for some vital function of the body and must be supplied by food.

Here is a brief description of what vitamins do for us. Vitamin A is essential for growth, for vision, and for healthy skin and mucous membranes. It is supplied by milk and milk products, eggs, liver, fruits and vegetables.

Vitamin B1 (thiamin) makes possible the proper use of carbohydrates and is required by the nerves. It is found in whole-grain bread, milk, vegetables, beans, nuts, and pork. Vitamin C prevents scurvy and is essential for healthy teeth, gums, and blood vessels. It is obtained from fresh fruits and vegetables.

A vitamin called niacin is needed to prevent pellagra, a disease that causes great suffering in undernourished people. It is supplied by meat, vegetables, and whole-grain cereals. Vitamin D prevents rickets. It is manufacutred in the body through the action of sun on skin. Vitamin D is now made synthetically in chemical factories and is often added to the milk you buy.

Other vitamins such as E and K and riboflavin have been isolated. Each one has a special duty to perform. That's why one should have a well-balanced diet to ensure an adequate intake of all vitamins.

WHY IS HAIR DIFFERENT COLORS?

Our hair has a very interesting structure. It develops from the horn layer of the skin, actually growing downward. It strikes root and then shoots upward through the layers of the skin.

Hair, like the epidermis from which it is derived, has a tissue of cells which form the "soil" in which it grows, and a horny shaft which is nourished and pushed upward by this "soil."

Among the cells at the root of the hair are cells that contain a pigment called melanin. These cells (like the others) multiply and move upward with the hair shaft as it grows. They die and leave the granules of pigment in the hair.

The pigment granules are all shades of brown, from a reddish color to a deep black-brown. The horn substance of the hair, in which the pigment is embedded, is yellow. The color of the horny material and that of the pigment granules mix together. And that's how all the different colors of human hair develop, from blond to black. Our genes, which we inherit, help decide what shades the pigment granules will be, and so what the color of our hair will be.

The average person has from 300,000 to 500,000 hairs in his skin. Blond persons have finer hair and more hairs than others. Dark persons have coarser hair and about a quarter less hair. Red-haired persons have the coarsest hair and the fewest hairs.

Your hair grows at the rate of about half an inch a month. And it grows at a different rate at various times of the day.

WHAT MAKES HAIR CURLY?

Hair is the slender, threadlike strands that grow out of the skin. There are many kinds of hair. Hair may be thick or fine, long or short. It may be white or colored. It may be straight, wavy, or curly.

Scalp hair is not the same among the many peoples of the world. Oriental people generally have hair that is quite straight. The Negro has tightly curled hair. The hair of Caucasians, or members of the white race, can be straight, slightly curly, or very curly.

So the color, curliness, and thickness of a person's hair are inherited. A person is born with a certain structure and type of hair. But there is something about the structure of hair that determines whether it will be curly or not.

Imagine that you cut across a shaft of straight hair and a shaft of curly hair, as you might cut across two tree trunks. If you were to look at the cut section of straight hair under the microscope, you would see that it is round. The cut section of curly hair is oval or flat. The flatter the hair is, the more easily it bends and the curlier it is.

The color of a person's hair depends largely upon a substance called melanin. Melanin is a pigment, or coloring matter. It is contained in the hair cells at the time they are formed in the root. It is the amount of this coloring in the cells that makes hair dark or light.

As people grow older, there is less and less melanin in the newly formed cells. That's why the hair gradually turns gray or white.

WHY DO WE GET SUNBURNED?

Most of us have no idea of the many ways in which light from the sun affects us. For example, sunlight destroys fungi and bacteria that may have settled on the skin. The action of sunlight on the skin produces a substance which contracts the blood vessels of the skin and thus raises the blood pressure. Ultraviolet light from the sun produces vitamin D in our bodies.

And one of the other things sunlight does to our skin is create the condition we call sunburn. There is a substance in the skin called histidin. Ultraviolet light from the sun transforms histidin into a substance that dilates the blood vessels, causing the skin to become red.

How do we get a "suntan"? The skin also contains a substance called tyrosin. Ultraviolet light acts on tyrosin and transforms it in the brown pigment called melanin. This melanin is deposited in the outside layers of the skin and makes it look "tanned." The melanin acts to protect the skin against further action of the light rays.

Because sunlight affects our skin and our body in so many ways, a person should be very careful in taking "sun baths." Did you know that if you expose only your feet to the sun's rays, you can raise the blood pressure, produce vitamin D that will go to the bones of the body, and so on?

Most people can't be bothered to do it right, but the healthiest way to take sun baths is very gradually. This would be exposing only one-fifth of the body for five minutes the first day, another fifth of the body for ten minutes the second day, and so on.

WHERE DO WARTS COME FROM?

Many people have superstitions about warts. They believe that if you handle toads, you get warts. Or that certain animals can pass them on to you.

None of this is true. You can't get warts by handling toads, and while dogs and cattle do have warts, there is no animal that passes warts on to human beings.

Warts are caused by a virus, which is a very small germ. This virus may be picked up by contact with others who have the virus.

A wart is usually a small raised area of the skin which is quite rough or pitted on the surface. It is flesh-colored or slightly darker than the normal skin. Since the wart is caused by a virus, it can be spread by scratching it and spreading the virus on the skin. That's why there are sometimes many warts on the skin.

Most warts disappear after a year or two. But there is really no guarantee that they won't spread or continue on and on. That's why it's a good idea to see a doctor about the warts.

In treating the patient for warts, the doctor usually uses some form of local medication, or he may inject special preparations into each wart. When there is constant pressure on a wart, such as those on the palms or soles, the problem becomes a bit more serious. The wart may become quite hardened and have to be removed.

HOW ARE BACTERIA USEFUL TO MAN?

When you say "bacteria," most people think of germs that are harmful and cause disease. But the fact is that there are over two thousand different kinds of bacteria, and most of them are either harmless or helpful to other forms of life—including man.

Bacteria cause the decay of dead plants and animals, both on land and in water. Without such bacteria the earth would be covered with dead matter. While eating, the bacteria break down the complicated substances in these organisms into simpler ones. The simpler substances are then restored to the soil, water, and air in forms that can be used by living plants and animals.

Bacteria play an important part in the digestive processes of man and other animals. There are a great many in the human intestine. As the bacteria eat, they break down foods. At the same time, they make certain vitamins, which the body then uses.

Bacteria are a vital link in the food chain that supports life. Some bacteria, called nitrogen-fixing bacteria, live in the soil and help change nitrogen into substances that plants can use. Man depends on such plants for food.

Bacteria are responsible for the fermentation process by which such products as cheese and vinegar are made. The same fermentation is also used in industry to make substances essential for paints, plastics, cosmetics, candy, and other products. It is also used to make certain drugs. In other industries bacteria are used in curing tobacco leaves, in tanning hides, in eating away the outer covering of coffee and cocoa seeds, and in separating certain fibers for the textile industry. So you see in how many ways bacteria are useful to man. And there are still many more ways they are used and will be used in the future!

CHAPTER 4
HOW THINGS ARE MADE

WHAT CAUSES CEMENT TO HARDEN?

Cement is one of the most useful materials in modern building. By itself, it is a soft powder. But when it is mixed with water and allowed to harden, cement can bind sand or gravel into a hard, solid mass.

Cement is used chiefly as an ingredient of mortar and concrete. Mortar is a mixture of cement, sand, and water. Concrete is the same mixture with gravel or broken stone added to it.

Modern cement is made by heating a mixture of limestone and clay or slag to a very high temperature. This mixture is heated until large, glassy cinders—called "clinkers"—are formed. The clinkers are then ground to powder.

When water is added to the cement powder, a very complicated chemical reaction takes place. The result is a durable artificial stone that will not dissolve in water.

What is this chemical reaction? What takes place that enables the cement to harden?

Chemists are still not sure of the exact answer. There are four major compounds in the cement, and it is believed that each of these compounds, when water is added, becomes crystals. These crystals interlock—and the result is the hardened cement.

The kind of cement that will harden under water is called hydraulic cement. An amazing thing is that the Romans discovered how to make a type of hydraulic cement in the 2nd or 3rd century B.C. by mixing volcanic ash with lime. This discovery was one of Rome's outstanding achievements.

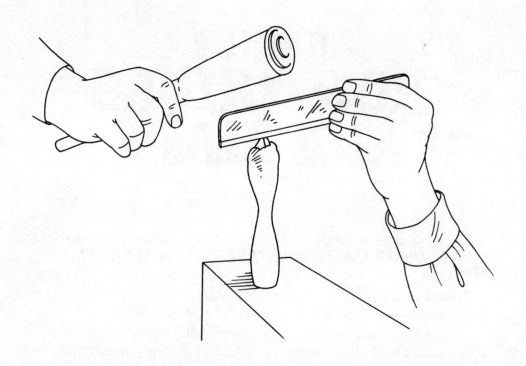

HOW CAN A DIAMOND BE CUT?

If a diamond is the hardest substance known, how can a diamond be cut? It is possible to do it because of two things: the structure of a diamond, and the way the cutting is done.

A diamond is highly crystallized carbon. The carbon atoms that make up a diamond have a geometrical arrangement. This means it is possible to cleave a diamond parallel to the planes in which the atoms are arranged and get smooth flat faces.

To cleave a diamond, a small diamond fragment is used as the cutting tool. A small groove is cut into one of the edges of the crystal. Then a thin, blunt-edged knife, or "cleaving iron," is positioned in the groove. A sharp blow is struck on this and the diamond crystal breaks apart. This is often done with large diamonds in order to remove flaws, or get a shape that provides more brilliancy, or to get more usable weight from the original stone.

In sawing or cutting a diamond, it is also necessary to go only in certain directions. A diamond is sawed by a thin phosphor bronze disk with its edge impregnated with diamond dust mixed in oil. In other words, it takes diamond to cut diamond. The saw revolves very fast, but it cuts the stone slowly.

The "facets," or little faces of a diamond, are ground on a high-speed cast-iron wheel impregnated with the same combination of diamond dust and oil.

Diamond cutting is a very skillful art which requires years of training.

WHAT IS A DETERGENT?

A detergent is a substance that makes things clean. So soap is really one kind of detergent. But when we say "soap," we usually mean a cleaning agent made from natural materials. And when we say "detergent," we usually mean a detergent made of synthetic materials.

Synthetic detergents are put together from many different chemicals by complicated processes. Petroleum, fats, coal tar, and other materials go into the complex formulas of these detergents. They are manufactured in chemical plants with special equipment. The ingredient in the detergent that does the actual cleaning is called the surface-active agent—surfactant, for short.

Surfactants can be made from a wide variety or raw materials, including petroleum, animal fats, and vegetable oils. The chemical processes involved are quite complicated. For example, animal fat may be treated with a series of different chemicals—an alcohol, hydrogen gas, sulfuric acid, and an alkali— to make one surfactant that is being used.

The surfactant must be mixed in a crutcher with other chemicals that help it remove dirt more thoroughly and keep the dirt from settling back on the cleaned material. Special bleaches, coloring, and suds stabilizers may also be added.

What has made synthetic detergents popular is that they produce suds in any kind of water, hard or soft, hot or cold; and they don't produce the curds that cause "bathtub ring." Today, about 90 percent of the packaged dishwashing and laundry products used in homes in the United States are synthetic detergents. Soap is still the most popular type of detergent for personal uses.

HOW ARE COLORS FORMED?

Light from the sun or from any very hot source is called white light. But that white light is really a mixture of light of all colors. This can be seen when light passes through a glass prism and is dispersed. We then see all the colors—red, orange, yellow, green, blue, and violet.

What creates the different colors? Color is determined by the wavelength of light. The wavelength of light corresponds to the distance between one crest and the next in a wave traveling on water. But the wavelengths of light are so small, they are measured in millionths of an inch.

The shortest visible waves are violet, with a wavelength of about 15 millionths of an inch. The longest are red, with a wavelength of about 28 millionths of an inch. In between are all the colors of the spectrum, and each shade has its own wavelength.

Most of the colors we see are not of a single wavelength, but are mixtures of many wavelengths. Purple is a mixture of red and violet; brown is a mixture of red, orange, and yellow. Different shades of any color can be made by adding some white light; for instance, a mixture of red and white is pink.

Why does a piece of cloth have a certain color when we look at it? When white light falls on an object, some wavelengths are reflected and the rest are absorbed by the material. A piece of red cloth absorbs almost all the wavelengths except a certain range of red colors. These are the only ones that are reflected to our eye—and so the cloth looks red.

WHAT IS A PHOTOELECTRIC CELL?

There are many types of photoelectric cells, and they are used for many things. One of the most familiar ones is when a door seems to open by itself when we approach it, as we often see at airports. This happens because our body blocks a beam of light and a photoelectric cell makes the door open.

Light is a form of energy. When light strikes certain chemical substances, such as selenium and silicon, its energy causes a push on the electrons in the substances.

If two different substances happen to be touching one another, some of the electrons may leave one substance and enter the other. Suppose an outside wire is attached to these substances so as to make a path for the electrons. Then, as long as light shines on the chemical substances, a continuous flow of electrons will take place through the substances and the wire.

Such a flow of electrons is an electric current. The entire path that the electrons travel along is called an electric circuit. A device that produces or increases the strength of an electric current when light shines on it is called a photoelectric cell.

Photoelectric cells are used in many ways. For example, solar batteries, placed in satellites and spacecraft, are a number of photoelectric cells connected together. In an exposure meter used on cameras, a dial is connected to a circuit that has a tiny photoelectric cell. The dial registers the amount of current flowing through the circuit. This tells how much light is shining on the cell.

CAMERA EXPOSURE METER

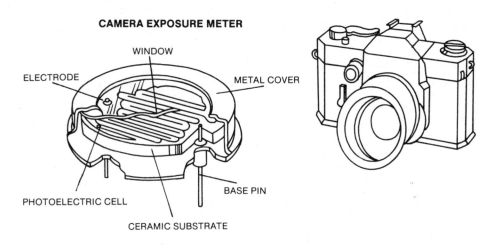

WINDOW

ELECTRODE

METAL COVER

BASE PIN

PHOTOELECTRIC CELL

CERAMIC SUBSTRATE

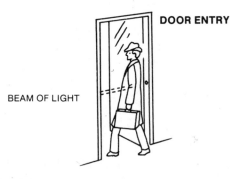

DOOR ENTRY

BEAM OF LIGHT

WHAT IS MUSIC?

Suppose you hit a wooden table with your hand. It makes a sound. Now suppose you hit a bell. It makes a sound. The second sound is called a tone. A tone is a single musical sound.

Music is the art of organizing tones into meaningful patterns of sound. We might call it the language of tones. Sometimes the language of music speaks to us in tones sounding after one another in melody. Or the tones could be sounding together in harmony.

When tones clash with one another, it is called dissonance. But this clashing is often full of meaning. What we call melody is given meaning by its rising or falling or moving straight ahead. It is also given meaning by its rhythm of beats and phrasing, its speed or tempo, and how loud or soft it is at any moment.

All of this sounds very technical, or mechanical. But it doesn't have to be understood or thought about for us to enjoy music. What music means to us can often not be put into words. We can feel that the music expresses joy or sorrow, gaiety, tenderness, love, anger—all kinds of things and feelings that words alone could never do.

Music can also be enjoyed just for its beauty, and not for what it is saying. We can get pleasure from even a single tone of voice, violin, horn, or some other instrument. We may love a beautiful melody for many years of our lives and always enjoy hearing it.

There are, of course, many forms of music, from the anthem to the symphony; and many types of music, from folk music to opera.

WHAT IS IRRIGATION?

Irrigation is the artificial application of water to land in order to increase the growth and production of plants.

In ancient times, irrigation was a natural process. For example, the annual flooding of the Nile River spread a thin layer of silt (mud) across the land. At the same time, the land received enough water so that crops could be grown.

Where irrigation was a natural process, people sometimes built canals, reservoirs, and drainage ditches. Floodwaters could then be directed where needed or stored for future use. This was the earliest form of man-made irrigation.

Today, in order to supply enough water for irrigation, costly dams and reservoirs are needed. Irrigation water may be so expensive that only good land can be irrigated profitably. Only such crops as vegetables and fruits can produce enough income to cover the costs.

The kind of irrigation used depends on the type of crops grown. Occasional flooding may be enough for hay, pasture, and the small grains. Furrow distribution (spreading water in ditches between rows) may be required for such crops as sugar beets and vegetables. In some cases, underground pipes with overflow standpipes are used.

Irrigation is not done only in dry lands. In Asia, irrigation is needed to raise rice, because rice fields must be covered with water at all times, until the rice crop is ready to harvest. In some parts of the world, supplemental irrigation is used. Pipes and sprinklers carry water to where it is needed most. This may save a valuable crop from serious damage by drought.

HOW IS CARBON-14 USED TO DATE OBJECTS?

All living things contain carbon. They also contain small amounts of carbon-14, a radioactive variety of carbon. Using carbon-14, scientists can determine the age of wood and clothing—in fact, anything that was once alive. Dating an object by means of carbon-14 is called radiocarbon dating. Radiocarbon dating is used to date objects up to 50,000 years old.

The rate at which a radioactive element breaks down is described by its half-life. An element's half-life is the time in which half the element's atoms break down.

Carbon-14 has a half-life of about 5,500 years. This means that about 5,500 years after a plant or animal dies, half the carbon-14 atoms present at the time of death are left. After 11,000 years, one quarter of the original carbon-14 atoms are left, and after 16,500 years, about an eighth of the original amount, and so on.

Suppose an old piece of wood is found in an ancient tomb. In the laboratory it can be heated and turned to carbon, or burned to release various gases, including carbon dioxide. The carbon or the carbon dioxide contains a few carbon-14 atoms. These atoms of carbon-14 are breaking down. With each breakdown a tiny particle is sent speeding out of the atom.

The carbon or the carbon dioxide is placed in a sensitive instrument—called a Geiger counter—which detects the particles given off by the atoms of carbon-14. From the number of particles given off, scientists can determine the amount of carbon-14 in the sample.

Scientists know how much carbon-14 is contained in an equal amount of wood from a living tree. From the amount of carbon-14 left in the ancient sample, scientists can tell its age. For example, if the ancient sample contained half the original amount, it would be about 5,500 years old.

WHAT IS AN AUTOPSY?

Quite often we read in the papers that an autopsy has been performed on a person who died from a disease, or from unknown causes, or who was murdered.

An autopsy is the examination of the body after death. Its purpose is to try to determine the cause of death. It is done by inspecting the organs of the body, and by making microscopic and chemical studies of pieces of tissue removed from the body.

Permission for an autopsy must be granted by the nearest of kin. It is similar to a surgical operation and is performed by medical personnel. An autopsy is performed in such a way that there will be minimal disturbance of the body. There is no visible evidence of an autopsy when memorial services are held for the person.

Why are autopsies done? Sometimes a doctor doesn't know the exact cause of a person's death. An autopsy can clarify this problem and might save someone's life in a future situation of the same kind.

An autopsy might reveal something about a disease that could be important to save the lives of surviving relatives. Sometimes an autopsy is done to identify a dead person who cannot be identified in any other way. An autopsy can help establish the time of death, which can be important when the person died from unknown causes or because of an act of violence.

Autopsies performed hundreds of years ago enabled man to begin to know about the human body and started the science of anatomy.

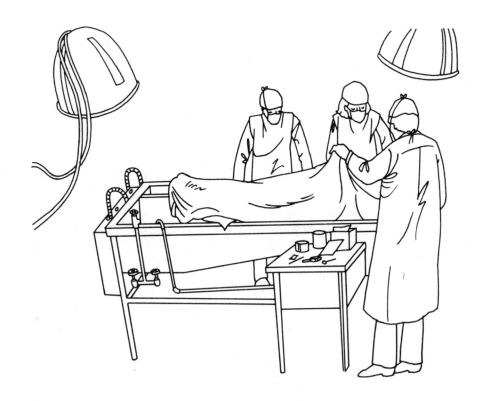

WHY DO GOLF BALLS HAVE HOLES?

To begin with, those are not "holes" in golf balls. They are small indentations, called dimples.

Like any sport, golf has certain rules and regulations. These also apply to the balls used. A golf ball is about half the size of a baseball or tennis ball.

But it just can't be any size. United States rules provide that a golf ball shall not weigh more than 1.62 ounces nor be less than 1.68 inches in diameter.

In Great Britain and most other Commonwealth nations, the rules allow for a slightly smaller ball.

Early in the history of golf, the balls were made of heavy leather, stuffed with feathers. Today the ball is made by winding strip rubber tightly around a core and covering it with a hard, rubberlike composition material.

Since one of the objectives of the game is to be able to hit the ball a long distance, and do it accurately, the cover of the ball is usually marked with the small indentations. It has been found by experts that these indentations (or what some people call "holes") make the ball fly straight when struck properly. It is also supposed to lessen wind resistance, and thus give greater carrying power to the ball.

ARE HORSES USED TO MAKE GLUE?

An "adhesive" is any sticky substance that holds things together. Adhesives are made out of a great variety of materials. The most modern kind of adhesives are synthetic resins, which are made from chemical raw materials.

Now, "glue" is also an adhesive, and it is made in a very special way. But many people call all adhesives "glue," and technically speaking, that is not correct.

Glue is an adhesive that is made from the protein "collagen." This protein is the chief thing found in the connective tissues of animals and fish. The chief way of obtaining the raw material for glue is by boiling animal hides and bones. And so that would include the bones and hides of horses (as well as other animals) when the animals have died. Actually, the bones of the animals make one kind of glue, and the hides make another.

The need for adhesives by man goes back to very ancient times. Primitive man used resins and plant gums to stick things together. But glue—the animal kind—has also been known for thousands of years. As far back as 1500 B.C., the Egyptians used glue to join pieces of wood.

The biggest change in the history of adhesives came with the development of the synthetic resins in the 1930's. They proved to be stronger and more durable than the natural adhesives, and they stood up against water, mold, and fungi as well. (Animal glue dissolves easily in hot water.) Today's synthetic adhesives are so strong that they are used in bonding the metal skins of some airplanes and missiles.

HOW CAN THE DISTANCE TO A STAR BE MEASURED?

Most stars are very large, yet to us they look like points of light. This is because they are so far away from the earth. In fact, while we can measure the distance to stars, we cannot really imagine how great that distance is.

The stars are so far away that the distance to them is measured in light-years, not in miles. One light-year is the distance that light travels in one year—nearly 6,000,000,000,000 (trillion) miles.

The closest star that can be seen with the unaided eye is just over four light-years away. Its name is Alpha Centauri. If the sun (which is a star) were as far away from the earth as Alpha Centauri, the sun would also look like a point of light.

Here is one way astronomers can estimate the distance to a star. They observe the star from two positions that are a known—and very large—distance apart. For example, they may observe the star from opposite sides of the earth. Or they may make observations a half year apart, when the earth is at opposite sides of its path around the sun.

When they do this, the star appears to have changed its position. This apparent change in position is called parallax. By measuring a star's parallax, an astronomer can calculate how far away the star is.

Because the stars are far away, they must be studied with telescopes. Through telescopes astronomers have observed and photographed hundreds of millions of stars. The most distant objects that can be seen through telescopes are thousands of millions of light-years away.

HOW ARE RAISINS MADE FROM GRAPES?

Raisins are small, very sweet grapes that have been carefully dried in the sun. There aren't too many regions in the world where grapes can be produced. The reason is that when the grapes are ripe, there must be many weeks of hot, rainless weather in which the grapes can dry.

There are regions near the Mediterranean, parts of Spain and Greece, and areas in Asia Minor that have the required climate; so do parts of southern Australia.

The San Joaquin and Sacramento valleys of California are ideal for making raisins, and lead the world in production. The drying season, from August to November, is hot and rainless, while the nearby mountains provide water for irrigation during the growing season.

In California, the grapes ripen in August. They are cut from the vines and allowed to lie in trays between the rows for from two to three weeks. Then they are put in boxes and allowed to dry some more. Then they are taken to the packing plant.

Here they are carried on conveyors to go through the process which prepares them for market. Special machinery removes stems and dirt from the grapes. Then the grapes are washed, steamed, or soaked in special solutions. Then they are dried and packed. About three-fourths of the original weight of the grapes is lost in drying them to make raisins.

Seedless raisins are made from the Sultana grape and from the Sultanina, both of which types grow in California.

WHAT IS LEATHER?

Leather is an animal hide or skin that has been tanned, or treated. The word "hides" is usually used to denote skins of large animals, as in cowhide or horsehide. The word "skins" is usually used for the smaller animals, as in goatskin or pigskin.

Cattle hides are the single most important source of leather raw materials. Calfskin leather is finer grained and lighter in weight that cattle hide. It is used for the most expensive shoes and handbags. The skin of any goat, old or young, is known as kidskin. Most suede leathers are kidskins buffed on the side that originally was next to the flesh.

The hide of the horse is used for shoes, jackets, and sports equipment. Pigskin leather is produced from hogs. The kangaroo provides the strongest of all leathers. It is used for track and baseball shoes. Alligator leather is used for shoes, handbags, wallets, and luggage. Even the skins of snakes and lizards are used as leathers for shoes, bags, and luggage.

Tanning turns animal hides and skins into soft, flexible leather. Tannin, the bark extract used in tanning, causes a chemical reaction. Different types of leathers are produced by slight changes in the chemical processes.

Before the hides are tanned, they must be preserved, or "cured." This is done in the packing house by salting the skins to prevent rotting. After the leather has been tanned, waxes, resins, shellac, or other chemicals are applied to make it shinier. Dyes are used to add color. The application of enamel paint called japan, or of plastics, gives patent leather its shiny surface. Suede leather is made when the underside of the leather is buffed or sandpapered to produce a nap.

HOW DO ESKIMOS BUILD IGLOOS?

To most of us the word "igloo" means a house built from snow. But "igloo," or "iglu," is the Eskimo word for shelter. An igloo need not be made of snow. It can be a tent, a schoolhouse, a church, or even a railroad station. Only the Eskimo of Canada and northern Greenland ever build snow houses, and these are used only in winter.

A snow igloo is called an "apudyak." It is made of frozen snow—not ice—which is carved into neat blocks. Snow has hundreds of air spaces, and this is what provides excellent insulation against cold weather.

An Eskimo can build a snow house quite quickly. Blocks of snow are cut about two feet long, eighteen inches high, and five inches thick. These are set on edge slanting inward to form a circle ten or twelve feet across. The blocks spiral upward and inward to form a dome. A small "breathing hole" is left open at the top of the igloo. Snow and ice platforms inside the igloo are covered with animal skins. Sometimes several snow houses are built together with connecting tunnels. Eskimo families can visit each other without stepping out into the cold.

Eskimos of Alaska never built snow houses. Their winter houses were partly underground. A white settler in Alaska once showed his young daughter how to build a snow igloo. His Eskimo neighbors were all amazed—they had never seen a snow igloo before!

HOW CAN A HELICOPTER HOVER IN SPACE?

A helicopter can fly in any direction: forward, backward, to the side, or straight up. It can even hover over a single spot. To understand how this is done, we must understand how a helicopter flies.

As the rotor blades of a helicopter slice through the air, the air beneath the blades has greater pressure than the air above them. This pushes the blades up and creates lift.

The wings of an airplane create lift in the same way. In fact, the rotor blades of the helicopter are really moving wings. The difference is that the whole airplane has to move forward in order to get lift, while the helicopter needs only to move its rotor blades through the air. This is what enables a helicopter to go straight up or down or hover over one spot.

In front of the pilot in a helicopter there is the "cyclic stick" or go-stick. He moves it in the direction he wants to go and the helicopter flies that way. The cyclic stick works by changing the pitch of one blade at a time as it passes one side of the helicopter. This means that one side of the disc—the circle made by the whirling blades—has more lift than the other, and the disc tilts.

When the disc is flat, the helicopter hovers because all the lift force is straight up, keeping the helicopter in the air. If the disc is tilted, most of the force is still up, keeping the helicopter in the air, but some of the force pushes slightly forward, backward, or to the side, and the helicopter moves in that direction as a result.

WHY DOES SILVER TARNISH?

Silver is a precious metal with remarkable qualities. It has been known and used by mankind before the dawn of history.

Silver conducts electricity and heat better than any other metal. Silver is the whitest of all metals. It reflects light better than other metals, which is why it is used as the backing material for mirrors.

Silver is also very easy to shape. Only gold can be worked with greater ease. Pure silver is very soft. Therefore, to increase its usefulness, small amounts of other metals are added to it. Sterling silver is 92½ percent silver and 7½ percent copper.

People who own objects made of silver often get annoyed because the silver begins to tarnish. The reason for this is that silver reacts very strongly to sulphur and many sulphur compounds.

With sulphur and hydrogen sulphide it forms black silver sulphide—and we notice this as the tarnishing or blackening of our silverware. The sulphur may be contained in certain foods, such as eggs, or by the tiny amounts of sulfurated hydrogen in the air. When buildings are heated by coal or oil, this can produce that effect in the air.

Silver is sometimes found in nature as native, or solid, metal. But more often it is combined with other metals and non-metals in mineral ores.

HOW IS BUTTER MADE?

Most butter sold in the markets today is made in creameries that buy milk and cream from many farmers.

After the cream is unloaded, it is pasteurized. Most butter is made from sweet cream. Sometimes a starter—lactic-acid-producing bacteria mixed with other organisms—is added to the cream. The starter causes the cream to ripen. Some coloring is usually added, too.

Then the churning begins. It is done by a revolving drum that shakes the cream back and forth until it is a grainy mass. Churning takes about an hour. The buttermilk is then rinsed off by spraying the butterfat with water. What is left is butter.

The churn is filled with water and rotated for a few seconds to wash the butter. Salt is sometimes added. The butter is then kneaded mechanically until it has the right texture and the proper amount of moisture. The butter is then smooth and firm and ready for packaging.

Butter is usually packed in bulk containers weighing about sixty pounds and shipped to central markets. There it is repackaged into smaller pound or quarter-pound boxes or bars.

Butter has been made by man since the earliest times. It is mentioned in the Bible many times. In Proverbs 30:33: "Surely the churning of milk bringeth forth butter." The Hindus used butter as long ago as 900 B.C., and it was often a part of their religious ceremonies.

WHY DOES SWISS CHEESE HAVE HOLES?

We enjoy different kinds of cheeses because they have different flavors. The flavor of most cheese develops while it is curing. Curing takes place when the cheese is held in storage under carefully controlled conditions of temperature and moisture.

During curing, harmless bacteria, yeasts, and molds are allowed to grow in or on the cheese to develop its flavor and odor. For example, many different microorganisms grow in cheddar cheese to give it a distinctive cheddar taste. Other kinds of bacteria and yeasts produce the special flavors of brick, Limburger, and Liederkranz cheese.

In the making of Swiss cheese, a special kind of bacteria is also used. It is called propioni-bacteria, and it gives Swiss cheese its sweet, nutty flavor.

It is the action of these bacteria that also gives Swiss cheese its odd appearance. While the cheese is curing, the bacteria give off gas. The gas bubbles form the round holes, or "eyes," of the cheese.

Other cheeses get their special appearance and flavor from certain molds. The blue veins in Roquefort and blue cheeses come from the mold *Penicillium roquefortii,* which produces the flavor and smooth body. A grayish-white mold, *Penicillium camemberti,* grows on the surface of Camembert and causes the creamy texture and that special flavor.

HOW DO SCIENTISTS DETERMINE OCEAN DEPTHS?

Finding the depth of water is called "sounding the depth" or "taking a sounding." In the old days, a weight was attached to one end of a rope. The rope was marked by a knot at every fathom (six feet). By counting the number of knots that went over the side before the weight hit bottom, one could determine the depth.

Today an echo sounder uses echoes of sound to explore the ocean floor. A device on board the ship sends out a sound signal which travels through the

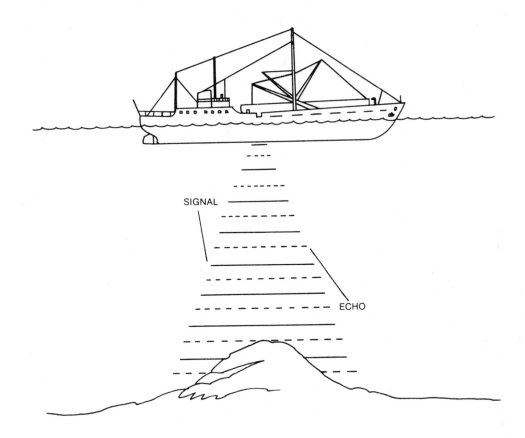

SIGNAL

ECHO

water at nearly one mile a second and is reflected—or echoed—back to an instrument. The deeper the water, the longer it takes for the echo to reach the ship.

In a modern echo sounder, high-frequency sound waves are beamed down from the ship. The instrument then records the echo as a dark mark on special paper. The paper is usually printed so that the depth can be read off in fathoms right away.

The echo sounder does more than just find the depth of the sea. It produces a continuous profile, or line, showing exactly what the ocean floor is like beneath the ship.

The soundings are so close together that the depth changes very little between one sounding and the next. If the ship passes over an undersea mountain, the echo sounder records the exact shape of the mountain. And if the bottom is flat, the record shows it as flat. The sounder does not miss a bump even a few feet high.

WHAT IS VIRGIN WOOL?

Soft woolen cloth is a favorite material for clothes and coverings all over the world. It keeps people warm, wears well, keeps its shape, and it can absorb moisture and still not feel damp to the skin.

The source of this fine fabric is chiefly the hairlike coat of the domestic lamb and sheep. This coat, like the fabric made from it, is known as wool.

The hairlike coat, or fleece, of some other animals also is wool, but usually has another name. Mohair comes from Angora goats and cashmere from Cashmere goats. Alpaca, llama, and vicuna come from animals of those names.

Wool is so valuable and useful that it is often used more than once. Manufacturers recover wool fibers from old clothing, rags, and manufacturing waste. They clean these and use them again.

To protect buyers, the United States government passed a Wool Products Labeling Act, which requires that products containing wool carry a label showing the amount of wool; the percentage of new, reprocessed, or reused wool; and the percentage of any fiber other than wool.

According to this act, "wool" means the fiber from the fleece of certain animals and not reclaimed. "Reprocessed wool" has been reclaimed from unused woolen materials. "Reused wool" has been salvaged from used woolen materials. And "virgin wool" means wool not used before in any way.

WHAT MAKES GASOLINE BURN?

Gasoline is very important in our lives because it is used as a fuel to make our automobiles go. Gasoline is a liquid fuel. It burns so rapidly and with such heat that it explodes.

Gasoline is a mixture of hydrocarbons or compounds made of hydrogen and carbon. These compounds are light liquids which boil at low temperatures. Carbon and oxygen are attracted to each other almost the way a magnet and iron are. When carbon combines with oxygen, burning takes place. This burning produces heat energy. When gasoline burns, the hydrogen joins with oxygen to form water vapor. The carbon and oxygen form carbon dioxide.

How does the burning of gasoline make a car go? The liquid gasoline is changed into a vapor and mixed with air by the carburetor of the engine. This mixture then flows into a cylinder where it is compressed by the piston moving up in the cylinder.

When the mixture of the gasoline vapor and air is compressed, a spark from a spark plug ignites the fuel. A great deal of gas is produced by the explosion (rapid burning), The pressure of the gas pushes hard on the piston and drives it down in the cylinder. The piston is connected to a crank which is free to turn. Thus, the push produced by the burning gasoline makes the crank go around. The crank is connected to the wheels and makes them turn.

WHY IS THERE LEAD IN GASOLINE?

Gasoline is a mixture of hydrocarbons. These are substances composed of hydrogen and carbon atoms.

The gasoline sold as motor fuel is usually a blend of several different hydrocarbon liquids. Special substances, called additives, are mixed with the gasoline to make it burn better.

At temperatures about 70 degrees Fahrenheit, gasoline turns from a liquid into a vapor. In an automobile engine, the gasoline is mixed with air and sprayed into the engine. The heat in the engine turns it into a vapor. A spark plug then sets off a spark that burns the mixture.

Sometimes the gasoline mixture may be ignited too soon. When this happens, the engine makes a sound, usually called a knock. There are two ways to reduce engine knock. One is to use a slow-burning gasoline.

The other is to put a chemical into the fuel to slow down the burning. The best-known chemical used for this is called tetraethyl lead, or simply ethyl. And that's why there is "lead" in gasoline.

Different kinds of gasoline are classed according to how much they are likely to knock in an engine. They are rated by an octane number. A gasoline with a high octane number will produce less knock than a gasoline with a low number.

Gasolines with an octane rating of 85 or more are considered good enough for most modern engines. Airplane fuel has an octane rating of 115 or more.

WHAT IS A SATELLITE?

In astronomy a satellite is a body that revolves around a larger body and is held captive by the larger body's attraction. Our moon is a satellite of the earth. The earth is a satellite of the sun.

Today when we say "satellite" we usually mean a man-made spacecraft circling the earth. Artificial satellites are sent into space for many purposes. Some are used for scientific research. Some send back information concerning the weather.

Some satellites relay television and radio broadcasts over long distances. Satellites may be used in navigation and map-making. Manned satellites give scientists information about how the human body reacts in a spacecraft.

Satellites can be of any size, from a tiny package of instruments to a huge balloon more than a hundred feet in diameter. They can weigh a few pounds or many tons. They can be shaped like balls, hatboxes, tin cans, bell buoys, and cigar boxes.

A satellite is launched at a velocity of 18,000 or more miles an hour. If no outside force acted on the satellite, it would travel off into space in a straight line. But the satellite cannot continue in a straight line because the earth's gravity attracts it, so the satellite is pulled into a curved path around the earth. The satellite is then in orbit.

Some satellites have orbits as near as 110 miles from the earth. Some have orbits as far as 22,300 miles from the earth. A satellite's orbit is chosen by scientists in advance, according to the task the satellite must perform.

WHAT IS A LASER BEAM?

The word "laser" is formed from the first letters of some long scientific words. The first two letters stand for "light amplification." The *s, e,* and *r* stand for "stimulated emission of radiation."

So a laser amplifies light. The laser can take a weak beam of light and make it into a strong beam. Some lasers produce beams so strong that they can burn tiny holes in strips of steel in less than a second.

Laser beams can travel long distances through space without spreading out and growing weaker. Because of this, they may become an important means of communication in the space age. Many uses have already been found for lasers in medicine, science, and industry.

Scientists think of light as traveling in waves. The distance from the crest of one wave of light to the next crest is called a wavelength. Light from the sun or from a lamp is a mixture of many wavelengths. Each different wavelength produces a different color.

A laser beam is made up of rays that are all exactly the same wavelength. Light rays in ordinary light are all traveling in different directions. The rays in a laser beam move in exactly the same direction. A laser beam does not spread out and grow weak.

All the rays in a laser beam are in step. That is, the crests of one light ray are lined up with the crests of all the other rays. When light rays are in step like this, they strengthen one another. That's why a laser beam is very powerful. A laser beam is started in the laser by a weak flash of light that has the same wavelength as the beam.

WHAT KEEPS YOU UP ON A MOVING BICYCLE?

Of course, when you go spinning down the street on a bicycle, you don't think of what forces are at work to keep you balanced upright. But there are at least two things that enable you to stay up on a moving bicycle.

One is the gyroscopic force. A gyroscope is a heavy-rimmed wheel-and-axle mounted so that its center stays in one place no matter how the gyroscope is turned. When the wheel is set spinning, it holds its position in space until an outside force changes it.

Your bicycle wheels, when they start spinning, react in the same way. They will stay in the same plane unless considerable force is used to change the direction. So gyroscopic forces tend to keep the bicycle upright.

The second thing is centrifugal force. Centrifugal effect pushes things away from the center of a rotating body. It is the force that pushes you against the side of the car when it turns sharply.

As you start to fall just a little bit on the bicycle, you turn the front wheel in the direction of the fall. The centrifugal force pushes you upright again. The path of the bicycle curves first to the right and then to the left as you compensate for each tendency to fall. In other words, you move the wheel, without thinking, in such a way that the centrifugal force will keep you upright.

WHAT IS INCENSE MADE OF?

Incense is a compound of gums and spices which produces a fragrant smoke when burned.

A resin is a substance that exudes from plants. A gum resin called frankincense, which comes from a certain tree, is the base of most incense, but other gum resins are used, too.

Incense has also been made from many other substances, including the bark, wood, and roots of trees, aromatic herbs, and plants, seeds, flowers, and fruits that give off an odor.

The custom of burning incense is ancient and found all over the world. One of its earliest uses was in religious ceremonies, to fumigate and purify animal sacrifices and fruit offerings at the altar. Among the Jews, following the Exodus, the burning of incense was a rite that was ordered to be done. It was part of the memorial worship.

Incense has been used by many peoples, including the ancient Egyptians, Romans, Hindus, Chinese, Persians, Aztecs, and Incas. The Catholic Church began to use incense extensively about the 5th century.

Today, both the Latin and Greek churches use it in worship. Among Roman Catholics, it is used chiefly at High Mass, and in processions, funerals, and the consecration of churches. The Anglican Church at one time stopped the use of incense, but then began doing it again in the middle of the 19th century. So the burning of incense has played a significant part in the religious ceremonies of man.

WHAT IS A DAM?

A dam is a barrier that holds back or controls the flow of water. Dams create lakes (called reservoirs) for storing water and supplying it as needed.

Dams help man to preserve and use water and land resources. A dam built in the right place can help prevent floods. The reservoirs behind dams store up drinking water for people and livestock. Dams provide water for irrigating dry fields. Electric power is produced at many dams by harnessing the power of falling water to turn machines called turbines, which drive generators.

There are several types of modern dams. Solid concrete gravity dams are designed so that the sheer weight of the solid concrete is enough to keep the dam from sliding or being overturned by the pressure of the water behind it. They are called gravity dams because they depend on the force of gravity to hold them in place.

Hollow concrete dams are made of concrete reinforced with steel. They require less concrete than solid dams, so they may cost less. Embankment dams are made of piles of earth and rock. They are also called earth-fill or rock-fill dams. Dikes and levees, which control floods along coasts and rivers, are embankment dams.

For almost every dam a spillway is important. A spillway is a sloping ramp or tunnel that is used to let water out of the reservoir gradually. Spillways are used to control the water level in the reservoir and to prevent water from suddenly overflowing the top of a dam.

Dams have been built on rivers and streams all over the world for thousands of years. The earliest known dam in Egypt is over 4,500 years old.

WHERE DO THEY GET IRON TO MAKE STEEL?

Basically, steel is an alloy of iron and carbon. Other ingredients may be included to give the steel different characteristics, such as hardness, toughness, and resiliency. But the most important material for steelmaking is iron. Iron does not usually occur in nature as a pure metal. Most of it is found combined with other elements in the form of iron ore.

In the United States, the area around Lake Superior—which includes Michigan, Minnesota, and Wisconsin—is the chief source of iron ore. This region at one time supplied about 80 percent of the iron ore used in the United States and Canada. Today, imports of iron ore from abroad have increased.

Lake Superior ores average about 51 percent iron. These high-grade ores are mostly near the surface of the earth. They can be mined simply by stripping away the covering layer of earth and scooping up the ore. The high-grade deposits have been running low, however.

The richest sources of iron are iron ores, such as magnetite, hematite, limonite, and siderite. Magnetite contains a higher percentage of iron than any of the other iron ores, sometimes as much as 72 percent. It is a black mineral in which three parts of iron are combined with four parts of oxygen. Sizable deposits of magnetite are found in the Adirondacks region of New York, in New Jersey, and in Pennsylvania. Magnetite is also found in Sweden, Norway, Russia, and Germany.

Hematite is the most common iron material now used as a commercial source of iron. It is a soft, sandy or earthy, red-colored ore. The best grades of hematite contain 70 percent iron.

HOW ARE BRICKS MADE?

Did you know that bricks are one of man's oldest permanent building materials? They were first used over 5,000 years ago.

All bricks are made from clay. Clay is a common mineral substance composed of very small rock particles. Some types of clay are formed by the disintegration of rocks by weathering. Clay is found over most of the earth's surface, often in lake and river beds.

Clay becomes slippery and plastic (easily molded) when it is wet. When it is dry, it becomes hard and stony. When clay is heated to a high temperature (about 850 degrees Fahrenheit), it changes chemically so that it no longer becomes plastic when it is wet.

This means that bricks of baked clay will not soften and lose their shape when they become wet. Bricks are baked, or burned, at 1600 to 2200 degrees Fahrenheit. At about 1000 degrees Fahrenheit the brick turns red and its color becomes darker as the temperature increases.

Basically, the manufacture of bricks has changed little since ancient times, except that machines now do most of the work. The clay is dug by power shovels. After drying, it is ground in mills and screened to get particles of uniform size. The clay is mixed with water into a stiff paste, then forced out under pressure through shaped nozzles, like a giant square-cornered strip of toothpaste. The strip is automatically cut into pieces of the proper size by knives or wires. The soft brick is then dried in heated tunnels and finally carried in small railroad cars to the kilns for firing.

The average brick can take a load of about 5,000 pounds a square inch before it is crushed.

HOW ARE SYNTHETIC FIBERS MADE?

Some fibers, such as cotton, wool, silk, linen, and hair, are natural. They are produced by plants and animals. Others, such as rayon, nylon, Dacron, Saran, are man-made. To understand how man-made, or synthetic, fibers are made, we have to know something about fibers.

Most fibers are made up of organic (carbon-containing) chemicals, such as are found in all living things. Some organic chemicals have a special quality. Their molecules (groups of atoms) attach themselves to one another somewhat like the links of a chain. This is called polymerization. Each fiber consists of millions of such molecular chains held together by natural forces called chemical bonds. Different fibers contain different numbers of each kind of atom in their molecules, and the atoms are arranged differently.

In making synthetic fibers, chemists take atoms of carbon, hydrogen, oxygen, and other elements, and combine them in such a way that new substances are created. The raw materials for synthetic fibers are coal, oil, air, and water.

Atoms from these raw materials are combined and arranged into long molecular chains called polymers. In other words, the polymerization is created by the chemists, instead of by nature.

These polymers are liquid when they are hot. They can be cast into solid plastics and films like Saran wrap, or they can be extruded through spinnerets (nozzles with tiny openings) to form filaments. From these filaments fabrics are made.

Of all the fibers produced every year, about one-fifth are synthetic fibers.

WHAT IS SONAR?

Let's start with an echo. When a sound bounces back from a large object, we call the returning sound an echo. When a radio signal is bounced back from an object, the returning signal is called a radio echo. Producing and receiving radio echoes is called radar.

A radar set produces radio signals. It radiates (sends out) the signals into space by means of an antenna. When a radio signal strikes an object, part of the signal is reflected back to the radar antenna. The signal is picked up there as a radar echo. A radar set changes the radar echo into an image that can be seen.

The word "sonar" comes from the first letters of "sound navigation ranging." Sonar is very much like radar. Sonar can detect and locate objects under the sea by echoes. Since radio signals cannot travel far underwater, sonar sets use sound signals instead.

Compared with ordinary sounds, sonar signals are very powerful. Most sonar sets send out sounds that are millions of times more powerful than a shout. These outgoing sound signals are sent out in pulses. Each pulse lasts a short fraction of a second.

Some sonar sets give off sounds that you can hear. Other sonar signals are like sounds from a dog whistle. Their pitch is so high that your ear cannot hear them. But the sonar set has a special receiver that can pick up the returning echoes. The echoes are then used to tell the location of underwater objects.

Sonar is used in searching for oil on land. A sonar pulse is sent into the ground. Echoes come back from different layers of soil and rock underneath. This helps geologists predict what may lie deep in the earth.

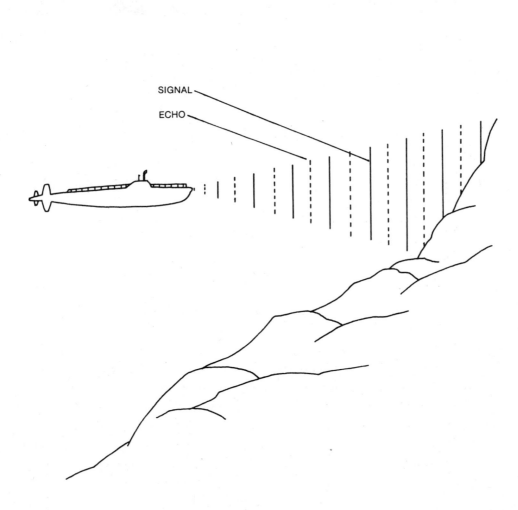

SIGNAL

ECHO

CHAPTER 5
HOW OTHER CREATURES LIVE

WHAT ARE EELS?

Eels are fish. Like all other fish, they have backbones, live in water, and breathe through gills. They are cold-blooded—that is, their body temperature varies with the surrounding temperature.

Most kinds of eels live in the sea. A few kinds live in fresh water for long periods of time, but they too spend part of their lives in salt water. All eels shed their eggs in salt water.

The eels most familiar to North Americans are the freshwater eels. They live in lakes, ponds, and streams from the Atlantic to the Mississippi River. Conger eels and moray eels, which live only in salt water, are found along the rocky coast of southern California and along the coast of the Gulf of Mexico, and along the Atlantic coast of the United States.

Eels eat many things, including dead fish and small living creatures. Eels are most active at night. Sometimes in late afternoon you can find tiny eels feeding in shallow salt water. When disturbed, they burrow rapidly into the sand.

The skin of eels feels smooth, for it is slimy with mucus. But there are tiny scales in the skin of freshwater eels and some others.

Freshwater eels migrate a long distance to spawn (shed their eggs) and they spawn in salt water, even though they live in fresh water. Few other fish can go from the ocean to fresh water, or from fresh water to the ocean, without dying. Biologists think that the body mucus helps protect eels against damage from this change.

Freshwater eels, moray eels, and some others, have a remarkable ability to recover from wounds that would kill other fish. A substance in their blood prevents possible infection.

DO HYENAS REALLY LAUGH?

There is actually a kind of hyena that is called the laughing hyena. It is the spotted hyena and is the largest member of the hyena family.

When this creature is on the prowl, or becomes excited by something, it utters a kind of eerie howl and chuckling gurgle that sounds like a laugh. But, of course, it is not "laughing" in the sense that human beings laugh. It is just making a shrieking noise that—to us—sounds like it is laughing.

The laughing hyena is a fierce-looking animal that stands about three feet high at the shoulder and is about six feet long. A big one may weigh as much as 175 pounds.

By day this hyena sleeps in a burrow or cave. When darkness falls, it comes out to seek food. Hyenas often hunt alone, but they may gather in packs around the remains of a kill left by lions or other beasts of prey. Their keen senses lead them to the kill, and they clean up all the remains.

The hyena is usually cowardly and sneaky, and it prefers to eat what others have killed and left. But it also lingers around camps and villages and sometimes attacks people sleeping in the open. It often follows herds of cattle or antelope. Closing in for the kill, it attacks a sick or crippled animal or else a very young or very old one.

The spotted, or laughing hyena, is an African species and it ranges from Ethiopia to the Cape of Good Hope. An unusual thing about the spotted hyena is that, unlike most animals, the female is larger than the male.

CAN SNAKES HEAR?

Snakes have no ears on the outside of their heads. This means that they do not hear airborne sounds as you do.

But snakes are sensitive to vibrations through the ground. So when a snake seems to "hear you coming," it is really feeling the ground shaking under your footsteps. Although a snake seems to have no sense of hearing, it more than makes up for it with other senses.

Most snakes can see very well. The eyes of snakes are always open, for snakes do not have movable eyelids. Snakes notice their prey more by movement than by shape or color. Snakes have a very keen sense of smell. They can recognize prey animals, enemies, and each other by odors.

Snakes also have another sense, related to both smell and taste, that human beings don't have. A snake can pick up chemical particles from the air, from the ground, or from some other animal or object, with the tips of its long forked tongue. The snake then thrusts these tips into a pair of openings in the roof of its mouth. These openings contain some highly sensitive nerve cells. And with these the snake can identify the chemical particles as food, enemy, friend, or whatever.

In fact, snakes have such a highly developed chemical sense that they can follow the trail of another animal like a well-trained hound. In addition, certain snakes—pit vipers and some boas and vipers—have a sense that no other animal has developed. They can sense a prey animal that is a little warmer or a little cooler than its surroundings.

This is a heat sense, and it enables these snakes to locate and strike a prey animal in the dark without ever seeing it!

HOW OFTEN DO SNAKES SHED THEIR SKINS?

There are over two thousand different kinds of snakes. They live on land, in the earth, in water, and in trees. So snakes vary quite a bit. But all snakes, young and old, shed their skins.

When they do this, even the film covering the eyes is cast off. During the process of shedding, the skin is turned inside out. The snake removes the skin by rubbing against rough surfaces. And snakes shed their skins several times a year.

The skin of a snake is scaly, and this is very important to them. In general, snakes have no legs, though a few types, such as the boas and pythons, have the remains of hind legs. These legs are imbedded in the muscles, and only spurs or claws show on the outside of the body.

It is the scales on the skin that enable snakes to move gracefully and even quickly. The broad scales on the underside can be moved forward in such a way that the rear edge of each scale pushes against some irregularity in the ground. When they are pushed back against these irregularities, the whole snake moves forward.

When the snake wants to move with great speed, it combines this with another method. This consists of swinging the body sideways into loops and, by pushing against any stone or plant it touches, gliding along the twisted path formed by the loops.

WHAT MAKES A RATTLESNAKE POISONOUS?

Scientists think that there are between 3,000 and 3,500 kind of snakes now living. Of these, 10 to 15 percent are poisonous kinds. They stun or kill their prey with venom. The rattlesnake happens to be one of the poisonous kind.

Rattlesnakes belong to a group of snakes called vipers, all of which are venomous. Rattlesnakes are pit vipers, and they get this name because of the two large pits on their heads. These pits are sensitive to the slightest change in temperature. They enable a viper to detect the presence of a warm-blooded animal even in the dark.

Vipers have a complicated type of venom system. Their fangs are very long. Each fang is set on a very short upper jawbone that can rotate. When a viper closes its mouth, the jawbone is rotated so that the fang lies lengthwise in the mouth and the mouth can close. When the mouth is opened for a strike, the jawbone is turned forward, bringing the fang at right angles to the throat.

The venom that vipers put into their victims with their fangs affects mainly blood cells and blood vessels. It may cause great swelling and bleeding. The venom of a few species, such as the South American rattlesnake, affects the nerves also.

There are 15 kinds of rattlesnakes, of various sizes and colors, in the United States and Canada. All of them have rattles at the tips of their tails. The "rattle" is made up of dry, horny rings of skin that lock loosely onto one another. When the snake shakes its tail, as it does when excited, these horny pieces of skin rub against one another. This results in a rasping or buzzing sound. This rattle helps the snake warn other animals away.

WHAT IS THE RATTLE OF A RATTLESNAKE MADE OF?

Rattlesnakes belong to a poisonous group of snakes called pit vipers. The pit vipers get their name from the two large pits on their heads, one on each side of the head, between the nostril and the eye. These pits are sensitive to the slightest change in temperature, so a viper can detect the presence of a warm-blooded animal even in the dark!

There are 15 kinds of rattlesnakes, and all of them have rattles at the tips of their tails. Even a young rattler has at least one round, shiny "button" at the tip of its tail.

The rattle is made up of dry, horny rings of skin that lock loosely onto one another. When the snake shakes its tail, as it does when excited, these horny pieces of skin rub against one another. This results in a rasping or buzzing sound. It serves to warn some other animal that it is too close for comfort.

Does a rattlesnake always give warning that it is going to strike by rattling? They usually do rattle when they become angry or frightened. But experts who have studied the habits of rattlesnakes report that this isn't always so. Many give no warning at all. So it isn't safe to depend on that warning rattle.

On the other hand, one can avoid being bitten by a rattlesnake by staying out of its range. A rattlesnake can only strike as far as it can raise its head. Even if it is coiled, it can strike only one-third to one-half its body length. And since rattlesnakes are rarely longer than six feet, one can be alert and stay out of its range.

WHY CAN'T THE OSTRICH FLY?

In the air the force of gravity is felt even more than when standing on the ground. This is because air gives little support to a creature's weight. Only small birds are able to fly by flapping their wings, because very large breast muscles are needed for this purpose.

A large bird does not have room for such muscles. And so the real giants among birds cannot fly at all. These include the ostrich, the rhea of South America, the emu of Australia, and a few others. All are much too heavy to fly. No bird can be truly a giant and still fly.

Is the ostrich really a giant? It certainly is! It is the largest of living birds. A full-grown ostrich is seven, and sometimes eight, feet tall. It weighs from 150 to more than 300 pounds!

But birds that cannot fly in some cases make up for this by having tremendous running speed. The ostrich is believed by some experts to be the fastest running bird. It has long, strong, thick legs and it can speed across the desert faster than the swift Arabian horse.

Some people claim they have seen ostriches run as fast as 50 miles an hour. But biologists believe that the fastest an ostrich can run is from 28 to 37 miles per hour—which is very fast, indeed.

The stride of the ostrich as it runs, moving one foot and then the other, can cover as much as 28 feet in a single leap.

WHAT DO HORNETS USE TO MAKE THEIR NESTS?

Several large members of the wasp family of insects are called hornets. They have thick bodies, usually black or dark brown, marked with brilliant white or yellow. This is why some of them are called "yellow jackets."

Hornets are social insects. They live together and build nests. If their nests are attacked, they become so angry that they sting the enemy very painfully. No wonder we have the expression "as mad as a hornet."

Hornets build large nests, sometimes a foot long, with a hole at or near the bottom. These nests are attached to branches of trees, or on bushes, or sometimes under the projecting roofs of buildings.

What are the nests made of? Paper. Yes—paper! We might say the hornets were the first paper-makers on earth. The paper is produced from wood pulp. The hornet collects it from boards or trees that have had the bark removed by accident or other means.

In collecting the pulp, the hornet goes backward, scraping off the pulp with its jaws and moistening it as it goes. This forms a round ball of paper pulp. The pulp is then spread into a sheet in building the nest.

Most people don't like hornets because they are afraid of their sting. And hornets do some damage to fruit. But, actually, hornets are a friend to man in destroying flies and other harmful insects.

HOW DO BEES STING?

First of all, not all bees sting. There are hundreds of different species, or kinds of bees, and many of them don't sting at all. When it comes to stinging by bees, what most of us are familiar with is the sting of the honeybee.

At the rear of the abdomen of the bee is the sting and other organs that surround it. The sting is quite a complicated thing. For one thing, it is an egg-laying apparatus, and actually part of its job is to deposit eggs.

The spearlike sting is made up of three pieces which surround a central canal. Connected to the base of the sting are two poison sacs. There are also two very sensitive, fingerlike projections. These tell the bee when the tip of her abdomen is in contact with the object she wishes to sting.

In the act of stinging, the spearlike sting is pushed outward and the poison sacs force the poison into the wound. It is this poison, in addition to the pain of the sting itself, that people want to avoid, for that poison can be very harmful to some persons.

Once the bee has inserted the barbed sting into the skin, it cannot be taken out easily. So when the bee flies away, her sting and its attached organs are pulled from her body, and she eventually dies.

If a bee does leave its stinger in a person's skin, it should be removed by scraping the stinger out with a fingernail or knife. Trying to pull the stinger out by its end may produce a squeezing of the poison glands if they are still attached and thus force more poison into the wound.

HOW DO WORMS CRAWL?

There are many different kinds of worms, but we will discuss the earthworm, the kind most familiar to us.

The body of the earthworm is divided into little rings, or segments, separated by grooves. So an earthworm belongs to the group known as "annelids." The name annelid means "little rings."

An earthworm stays underground most of the time, tunneling through soft, damp topsoil and feeding as it goes. It produces a slime that makes travel easy. An earthworm burrows along, using two sets of muscles.

One set of muscles runs around the body, with one muscle in each segment. When the segment muscles tighten, the body becomes longer and thinner. The front end is pushed forward. The second set of muscles runs lengthwise along the body. When these muscles tighten, the segments are pulled up close together. The body shortens.

An earthworm is like a tube within a tube. The long, segmented body is one tube. Within this is the long digestive tube through which the food passes. The digestive tube is open at both ends. Food passes in at one end, and the undigested remains pass out at the other.

In heavy or deep soil a worm tunnels by swallowing the soil. This method of moving is also a way of eating, for there are decaying bits of plants and animals in the soil. These are digested as the soil passes through the digestive tube.

This activity of swallowing soil and bringing it up to the surface plays an important part in turning over and enriching the soil. Scientists say that in each acre of land earthworms turn over ten to eighteen tons of soil each year.

HOW ARE FISH ABLE TO SMELL THINGS?

It probably surprises many people to learn that fishes can smell things just as other creatures can. Fishes smell with their noses.

There are two pairs of nostrils in a fish. That is, each nostril has two openings, which are called pits. One opening is in the front. The other is directly behind it. The two are separated by a small flap. The nostril can be in a number of different locations on the face. As is true with everything about fishes, there are many variations.

A current of water enters and leaves each pit. It flows in the front one and out the rear one. As the water flows, it stimulates the sense cells that tell the fish about odors. Many fishes have a keen sense of smell. They can detect the very smallest traces of substances.

In fact, the sense of smell may be important to fish in helping them find their way home. As we know, salmon return to their original home to spawn. How do they do it? Scientists believe that perhaps salmon can tell their childhood stream by its odor.

Researchers have trained salmon to distinguish 14 different kinds of colors. Some fish could tell the difference between water from two creeks. But if their noses were plugged up, they couldn't tell.

In other experiments a large number of salmon were taken out of their home stream. One half had their noses plugged; the other half didn't. Those with plugged noses got lost. The others found their way home again.

DO ALL FISH LAY EGGS?

Most fishes lay eggs and these eggs are fertilized outside the body. Fishes that emit eggs are described as oviparous. But some fishes give birth to living young. These are described as viviparous.

Among the viviparous fishes are guppies, platies, swordtails, and mollies.

The eggs are fertilized inside the body of the female and grow into baby fish there. At the appropriate time, they are born. In platies it is 21 days after fertilization.

The number of eggs that are laid and fertilized vary a great deal from one kind of fish to another. Some fishes expel their eggs and then abandon them, showing no more interest in them. These kind of fishes lay great numbers of eggs. Those fishes that watch over their developing young lay far fewer eggs.

Fishes also lay two types of eggs. One type floats and the other sinks. Eggs that float are called pelagic eggs. They are usually tiny and transparent and do not have much yolk. Eggs that sink are called demersal eggs. They are usually heavier and yolky.

As an example, herring lay demersal eggs and show no care for these eggs. They may deposit 20,000 to 40,000 eggs. Cod, on the other hand, lay pelagic eggs. An average-sized cod can lay one hundred million eggs!

Mackerel lay 400,000 to 500,000 eggs in a season, but they never lay more than 50,000 at a time. Large halibut can lay over two million eggs!

Eggs vary in size, too. Herring eggs are 1/25-inch in diameter. Cod eggs are about 1/15-inch. Halibut eggs are ⅛-inch. Eggs that are guarded until the young are larger have greater chance for survival. But billions and billions of fish eggs are eaten by other creatures.

HOW DO JELLYFISH REPRODUCE?

One of the most common jellyfishes in the world is the moon jellyfish. It has long, milky-looking threads streaming down from its round, cuplike body.

On the upper side of a fully grown moon jellyfish there is a pink or orange pattern like a four-leaf clover. The four "leaves" are the reproductive organs. In male jellyfish they produce sperm cells, which are released through the animal's mouth into the water. In female jellyfish the reproductive organs produce eggs. The eggs remain inside the body until they are fertilized, or joined, by sperm cells from the water.

The eggs develop in four long, trailing folds that hang down from the mouth. When the eggs hatch, the young settle on the bottom of the ocean. They develop into a shape very different from the parent animal. They become polyps (which means "many feet").

The young polyp catches food with its tentacles and grows for several months. Then something strange starts to happen. The polyp begins to develop grooves. Gradually, the polyp begins to look like a stack of fringed saucers.

One by one the saucers pinch off from the polyp and swim away. Each becomes a separate little jellyfish.

Apparently the jellyfish way of life and of reproducing works out quite well. Jellyfish have been doing this for more than 600,000,000 years! They are among the oldest forms of life on earth and have changed very little.

HOW DO FISH REPRODUCE?

Most fishes lay eggs. They either sink or float in the water. The outside shell of the egg is a transparent membrane. Inside, the egg itself is made of yolk and of protoplasm. Protoplasm is the living matter that becomes the future fish. The yolk, like the yolk of a chicken egg, nourishes the developing fish.

The egg cell is fertilized by a sperm from the male. The sperm swims into the egg cell through the shell, or membrane. The membrane has a small opening in it, just above the cell. Sperm swimming to the egg can get into the egg only through this opening. If sperm pass through, the egg is fertilized by one of the sperm.

Then life within the egg begins. The cells begin to divide until they form a thin sheet that encloses the entire yolk. The sheet then gradually begins to take the shape of the future fish. There is a bulge where the head will be, muscles appear as small blocks, the tail bud appears, and so on.

This embryo fish continues to grow inside the egg. After a certain number of days, the shell softens. The embryo hatches out of it. It is free to drift and to grow into an adult fish.

We have been discussing eggs that are laid and fertilized outside the body. Fishes that shed eggs are known as oviparous. But other fishes are viviparous, which means that they give birth to living young. Among such fishes are guppies, swordtails, and mollies.

The eggs are fertilized inside the body of the female and grow into baby fish there. At the appropriate time they are born.

DO FISH EVER SLEEP?

Can you sleep with your eyes open? No, you have to close your eyelids to go to sleep. And that's why most fishes do not sleep as we do. They do not have eyelids that they can close. But they do rest when the light dims. Some fish, such as the triggerfish, even lie down on their sides to rest.

The eye of a fish is similar to ours in many ways. But there are differences because a fish sees in water, while we see in air. As in people, there is an iris that surrounds the lens in fishes. The opening in the iris is called the pupil. The pupil of the eye always stays the same size in most fishes.

This means it does not close in bright light or open in dim light, as ours does. So if we turn on a bright light, the fish may be dazzled. It can't close out some of the light, as we can. However, a few fishes do have pupils that can narrow. By the way, fishes can't shed a tear, for they have no tear glands. Their eyes are kept moist by the surrounding water.

In most fishes the eyes are placed on each side of the head. Fishes see different images out of each eye. They have a large field of vision on both sides. Their field is much larger than ours. They can see in front, behind, above, and below themselves. Just in front of its nose a fish can focus both eyes on the same object.

Experiments have shown that some fishes can see colors. They can also distinguish between red and green, and probably between blue and yellow. However, not many species have been tested. So we cannot say that all fishes can see color. Also, there are many differences among the species.

WHAT IS A VULTURE?

The vulture is a large bird of prey. The word "vulture" has become a kind of symbol for creatures that feed on other animals.

Vultures belong to the same order of birds as the falcons, hawks, and eagles. There are five vultures to be found in North and South America. They are the turkey vulture, the black vulture, the king vulture, the California condor, and the South American condor.

All vultures feed on carrion (dead animals), which is why most people don't like them. Actually, these large birds are very graceful in flight, and one can admire the way they glide about in the air. But when a vulture discovers a dead animal, it swoops down, is joined by other vultures, and the birds tear the animal apart with their hooked beaks.

The South American condor is the only member of the vulture family that sometimes kills animals for food. It eats eggs, young sea birds, and young mammals. It also eats any dead animals that it can find.

How do vultures discover dead animals they eat? Many experiments have been made to get the answer. It is known that vultures have much better eye-

sight than human beings have. They can see small things from great distances. But they have hardly any sense of smell. So we still don't know exactly how they do it.

By the way, the North American vultures are quite welcome during stock-killing time on western ranches. They gather in numbers and save the rancher the labor and expense of getting rid of the unused parts of the animals killed.

WHEN DID HORSES COME TO NORTH AMERICA?

This question should really be: when did horses come *back* to North America? The horse developed into its present form in North America millions of years ago.

From time to time during their long history, horses traveled over land bridges from their North American homeland. They spread into South America, Asia, Europe, and Africa. On all these continents they evolved into numbers of different species. But during the Ice Age all the horses living in the Americas became extinct. At the dawn of recorded history there were no horses in North America. Horses then lived only in Europe, Asia, and Africa.

It was the Spanish conquistadores who brought horses back to America. In 1519 Hernando Cortes carried 16 horses with him when he sailed from Havana for the conquest of Mexico. De Soto brought more than two hundred horses with him when he landed in Florida in 1539. He still had most of them when he pushed on across the Mississippi River in 1541. And Coronado, exploring the Southwest at the same time, had one thousand or more horses in his expedition.

Spanish missionaries and settlers followed the explorers, bringing still other horses with them. At first the Indians were frightened by the horses, for they had never seen such beasts. But they quickly discovered how useful horses could be. Soon they began to steal horses from the Spaniards and to capture runaways. Tribe after tribe acquired horses.

Possession of the horse changed the whole way of life for many western Indian tribes. Horses made it possible for them to move from one campground to another quickly and easily. Horses also allowed them to follow the bison herds and kill all they needed. Plains Indians also used horses in warfare against one another and against the invading white man.

HOW DO SCIENTISTS KNOW ANIMALS ARE COLOR BLIND?

To find out whether animals can see colors, scientists have conducted certain experiments. All they can say is that, according to the results of these experiments, certain animals cannot see colors.

Let's consider dogs, for example. Dogs were able to be trained so that their mouths watered (salivated) when definite musical notes were sounded. This was because when those notes were sounded, the dogs would be given food. Then the same kind of experiment was tried with different colors. It was impossible to make dogs tell one color from another as signals for food. Conclusion: dogs are color blind.

A similar type of experiment was made with cats. An attempt was made to train different cats to come for their food in response to signals of six different colors. But the cats always confused their color with shades of gray that were shown. So it is believed that cats are color blind.

We know that monkeys and apes can see colors because certain experiments prove it. They have been trained to go for their meal to a cupboard, the door of which was painted a certain color, and they wouldn't go to doors painted with other colors—and which had no food.

But even scientists say that the evidence that most animals are color blind is not complete. Maybe more tests will reveal things we don't know about animals. For example, tests were made that showed that horses are able to tell green and yellow from any shade of gray and from one another. But they don't seem to be very good at recognizing red or blue as colors.

HOW DO WE KNOW BATS USE RADAR?

Most bats are active only at night. They come out at night to find food. For centuries men who studied bats wondered how they found their way in the dark. How could a bat with no light to see by find a flying insect and catch it in flight?

Many people used to think that bats had unusually keen eyesight and could see by light too faint for human eyes to detect. Scientists now know that a bat's ability to navigate depends not on its eyes, but on its ears and vocal organs.

Way back in the 1780's an Italian zoologist named Spallanzani did an experiment. He blinded some bats and released them into a room crisscrossed with silk threads. The bats flew through the maze without touching the threads. When he plugged their ears, they became entangled in the threads. Spallanzani felt that bats used their ears rather than their eyes to find their way in the dark.

In 1920 a scientist suggested that bats sent out signals that were beyond the range of human hearing. Such sounds are called ultrasonic. In 1941, two other scientists decided to use a new electronic instrument that detected ultrasonic sounds in an experiment with bats.

The machine showed that the bats were uttering high-pitched cries, and that they were constantly squeaking as they flew through a maze of wires that had been set up in the dark. When they taped the bats' mouths shut, the animals blundered badly.

A bat sends out signals—high-pitched squeaks that bounce off anything in its path. A sound is bounced back, or reflected. It is an echo. The bat uses echoes to locate things in the dark.

DO POLAR BEARS HIBERNATE?

The word "hibernate" comes from the Latin and means "winter sleep." Many people think that certain animals hibernate because the weather gets cold where they live. And since polar bears live where it's very cold, they must hibernate.

But animals who hibernate do it because their food supply becomes scarce in winter. They do not store up a food supply for the winter. Instead, they lay up a reserve supply of fat on their body. Then the hibernating animal sleeps through the cold winter, living on the fat it has stored up in its body.

During this sleep, all life activities nearly stop. The body temperature goes down, the breathing is slow, the heart beats faintly. Do polar bears do this?

The answer is no. They do sleep more in the winter than in summer, but their sleep is not the deep sleep of hibernation. Their temperatures and breathing remain normal. They sleep in hollows or caves in the ice or snow. During warm spells they may even venture forth for a day or so.

Female polar bears do more sleeping in winter than the males. They go into dens and are often snowed under for weeks. The cubs are born during this winter sleep. The cubs are often very small, weighing no more than six or eight ounces at birth. So the mother bear nurses them and cares for them for several months during the winter.

Hibernating animals are awakened in the spring by the change in temperature, moisture, and by hunger. They crawl out of their dens and start eating again.

WHY DO OPOSSUMS CARRY THEIR YOUNG?

Opossums belong to a group of animals called marsupial. The females of this troup have pouches on the underside of the body in which the young develop.

An interesting thing about opossums is the fact that the young are so small. You could put all of the 5 to 18 babies in a tablespoon when they are born! At birth they are blind, hairless, and practically shapeless.

Because they are so small, and still quite helpless, the mother opossum carries her young. They ride on her back. She brings her tail up and they wrap their tails around it. When they are about three months old, they leave their mother; and at one year they are ready to raise families.

The babies climb into their mother's pouch, and attach themselves to the milk glands. When they are a month old they begin to poke their heads out of the pouch. A few weeks later they crawl out for short periods of time.

Opossums spend a lot of time in trees, hunting and eating. They like to eat upside down. To do this, they wrap their tails around a branch, hang down, and grasp their food by all four feet.

Opossums eat small mammals, insects, small birds, eggs, poultry, lizards, crayfish, snails, fruit of all kinds, corn on the cob, mushrooms, and worms. At night opossums invade orchards for fruit and henhouses for poultry and eggs. So man doesn't exactly like all their eating habits. But opossums do help farmers by killing mice and insects.

CAN A BUTTERFLY SMELL?

It may surprise us, but butterflies and moths have keen senses of sight, smell, and taste. The organs of taste in most butterflies are in the mouth, which is what you would expect. But most organs of smell in butterflies are on the antennae. And there are some butterflies that smell things through "noses" on their feet!

Many butterflies have odors, or scents, which they use for two purposes. One kind of scent is used to attract the opposite sex; the other is used to drive away enemies.

The scents of male butterflies come from scales in pockets on their hind wings. During courtship a male monarch butterfly may scatter these scent scales over the female. The scents of many male butterflies resemble those of flowers or spices and are often pleasant to humans.

Female butterflies produce their scents in special glands in their bodies. Most of these female odors are disagreeable to the human nose.

Did you know that the taste organs of a butterfly are far more sensitive in some ways than that of humans? They are far more sensitive to sweet things than our tongues are. Their chief food is flower nectar, which is a sugar solution, and they are easily able to find it. When a butterfly finds nectar in a flower, it uncoils its long, hollow "tongue" and sucks in the liquid.

Butterflies are able to see colors very well. They can even see certain ultraviolet colors that the human eye cannot see.

WHY DO A CAT'S EYES GLOW IN THE DARK?

People who own and love cats consider them to be sweet little creatures and wonderful pets. Which they are. But cats are members of a family of animals of a very special kind. These include tigers, lions, leopards—and, of course, the domesticated cat.

No matter where they live, no matter what their size and appearance, all cats are alike in many ways. All have bodies adapted for hunting and killing. All are highly specialized beasts of prey.

One of the things that helps a cat to be a good hunter is its eyes. The cat's eyes are adapted for seeing in the dark, since it does most of its hunting at night. During the day the pupils contract to slits, or very small openings. But at night they open wide, letting in every bit of light possible.

The backs of the eyes are coated with a substance like polished silver. It reflects every bit of light that comes into the eye. That is why a cat's eyes shine like glowing lanterns if you point a flashlight toward them at night.

What are other things about the cat that make it a great hunter? In the front of its mouth the cat has four long, pointed canine teeth—deadly weapons for biting and tearing flesh. On its feet the cat has an arsenal of needle-sharp, curved claws. To follow its prey silently, there are soft pads cushioning the bottom of its feet. And the cat has unusually keen sight, hearing, and smell.

WHY DO CATS HAVE WHISKERS?

The cat family includes everything from the small domestic cats we keep as pets to Siberian tigers weighing 600 pounds or more. But no matter where they live, no matter what their size and appearance, all cats have bodies adapted for hunting. All are highly specialized beasts of prey.

A cat has whiskers to help it perform in this way. When a cat is on the prowl, and its eyes and ears are not receiving any information to help it, or are busy, whiskers help the cat learn more about its surroundings.

For example, when a cat puts its head into a dark hole, the whiskers touch the sides of the hole and tell the cat where the boundaries of the hole are. Or the whiskers may brush against the body of a mouse and tell the cat at once that its prey is there.

So the long hairs of the cat's whiskers are what it depends on to know where it is, what's there, when the other sense organs, such as sound and smell and sight, can't provide that information.

But cats do have very keen senses. Their hearing and sense of smell are highly developed. They have keen eyes and they are directed forward (as ours are). This allows the cat to focus both eyes on the same subject at the same time and to judge its distance.

The cat's eyes are also adapted for seeing in the dark. During the day the pupils contract to slits, but at night they open wide to let in every bit of light possible. The backs of the eyes are coated with a substance that reflects every bit of light that comes into the eye.

HOW DID THE HIPPOPOTAMUS GET ITS NAME?

There are many amazing things about this beast, including its strange name. The word "hippopotamus" means "river horse." The animal got this name partly because it spends much of its time in the water. And it may have been called a horse because of its great size or its wide nostrils or its little horselike ears.

Actually, the closest living relative of the hippopotamus is the pig! The hippo is far larger than any horse. A big hippo can be twelve feet long and weigh up to four tons.

The hippo has the biggest mouth of any mammal except the whale. It has two tusks in the upper jaw and four in the lower. When it attacks, it can kill a smaller animal with a single bite. Usually, however, the hippopotamus would rather hide than attack. Most of the time it will run to the water to hide.

A hippo can run as fast as a man. In the water it can drop out of sight like a stone or it can float. When the hippo floats, only its bulging nostrils and eyes and its little ears show above the surface. It is almost hidden, but it can still breathe, smell, see, and hear.

When it sinks, the hippo closes its nostrils to keep the water out. It can walk around on the bottom and gather the juicy water plants it likes to eat. It can easily stay under for eight or nine minutes!

The hippo has an appetite to match its size. A big hippo that lives in a zoo may eat about one hundred pounds of food every day. A herd in the wild will eat many kinds of river plants and grasses. Hippos usually feed at night and rest during the day.

WHAT IS A MAMMAL?

Mammals are the most advanced of all the different classes of animal life. They are also the animals that we know best, and include dogs, cats, rabbits, horses, cows, pigs, elephants, bears, mice—and human beings. And there are hundreds and hundreds of other kinds of mammals.

Mammals have certain characteristics, some of which are shared by other creatures, some of which are not. Mammals are vertebrates—animals with backbones. (So are fishes, reptiles, and birds.) All mammals have lungs and breathe air. (So do birds, reptiles, and many amphibians.) All mammals are warm-blooded. (So are birds.)

All mammals, except two primitive types that lay eggs, give birth to living young. So do many fish, reptiles, insects, and other animals.

There are two important characteristics that set mammals apart from all other animals. They are the only animals that possess true hair, or fur. They are the only animals that produce milk. The word "mammal" comes from the Latin word *mamma,* which means "breast." All female mammals nurse their young with milk that comes from glands, usually called breasts, on their bodies.

Mammals have certain other characteristics. The mammal's lungs and heart are separated from its stomach and intestinal tract by a wall of muscle called the diaphragm. The mammal's lower jaw consists of a single bone on each side. And—most important of all—mammal brains are much more highly developed than the brains of any other animals.

WHAT IS A SLOTH?

When we say a person is a "sloth," we mean he is sluggish and lazy. What we are saying is that he takes after the sloth, an animal that is very sluggish and sleeps 18 hours a day.

Sloths are strange-looking animals found in Central and South America from Nicaragua to Brazil. They live in trees and are never seen away from forest areas. Sloths are mammals and are related to anteaters, armadillos, and aardvarks.

There are two types: three-toed and two-toed sloths. The three-toed sloths have three toes on each foot. The two-toed have two toes on their front feet and three on the back.

They use their toes and claws to hang from branches in an upside-down position. At night they inch slowly along the branches in search of tree leaves and twigs, which they eat.

Sloths sleep in the trees, on the upper side of a strong limb. Sometimes they crawl over the ground, and where there is a stream or a lake they jump in without fear and swim easily.

Sloths are very low in intelligence, because their brain is very small. Their body temperature is also the lowest of any mammal, and in fact they sometimes behave more like cold-blooded animals than warm-blooded animals.

The fur of a sloth is gray and shaggy. Sometimes algae grow in the fur, and this gives it a greenish tinge. But this actually helps sloths — because the green color helps them stay unnoticed by eagles, jaguars, and other animals that feed on them.

WHEN DID REPTILES FIRST APPEAR?

The first reptiles walked on the earth about 300,000,000 years ago. In those days the largest animals on land were amphibians. Their eggs were laid in water.

The first reptiles looked like amphibians, but the big difference was that their eggs could hatch on land. The young had lungs and legs, and could breathe air. They walked on damp ground in forests, and probably fed on insects.

Later on, reptiles became larger and stronger. Some looked like lizards and some like turtles. There were also reptiles with short tails, thick legs, and large heads.

One group of early reptiles were very important because of their descendants. They looked like lizards that were about three feet long, but they walked on their hind legs.

From these creatures many new types of reptiles developed. Some were true reptiles with wings. One group developed feathers and warm blood—they became the first birds. Other types that developed were crocodiles and the first dinosaurs.

At one time, all the types of reptiles that existed dominated life on earth. But after millions of years, many of the ancient types of reptiles became extinct. There are many theories that try to explain why this happened. The chief explanation seems to be that changes in the earth and its climate made it impossible for them to live on. Swamps dried up and they couldn't live on dry land. Their food disappeared. Climates became seasonal, shifting from summer heat to frost in winter. Most reptiles could not adjust to these changes, and those that couldn't died out.

HOW DO TURTLES BREATHE UNDERWATER?

Many turtles spend all or most of their lives in fresh water. They may live in swamps, ponds, running streams. They come up on dry land to sun themselves or lay eggs. How do they breathe when they are in the water?

Turtles have lungs and breathe air. They do not get oxygen from the water as fish do. So turtles have to fill their lungs with air to enable them to stay underwater.

They cannot do this by moving their ribs, as we do. Their ribs are firmly fixed to their hard shells. Turtles fill their lungs in another way. A turtle has two special sets of belly muscles. One set pulls the other body organs away from the lungs. Then a second set of muscles pulls the organs against the lungs, forcing the air out. One deep breath may last a land or sea turtle several hours.

Some freshwater turtles may remain underwater for several days without surfacing. They can do this because they use up very little oxygen while lying still on the bottom.

A few kinds of turtles have a special lining in their throats or in the cloaca. This is the opening through which wastes and other substances leave the body. This lining can take oxygen from the water, as the gills of fish do. Such turtles still need to come up for air, however.

A soft-shell turtle can breathe without moving from its shallow river bottom. Its neck is long enough to reach up to the surface of the water.

WHERE ARE BLUE WHALES FOUND?

First, what are blue whales? Well, to most of us, whales are whales. We are not aware that there are many different kinds of whales.

Scientists divide whales into two groups: Odontoceti and Mysticeti. Odontoceti means "whales with teeth." Mysticeti means "moustached whales." These whales have "moustaches" of baleen, or whalebone, hanging from the roof of the mouth. Baleen is a fibrous, horny substance, fringed along the inner edges. Using their baleen, these whales strain huge quantities of small food out of the water.

The baleen whales are the largest animals ever to live on earth. Bigger than the dinosaurs? Yes! The blue whale, which is the largest of this type, may be 100 feet long and weigh more than 120 tons—and even the biggest dinosaur didn't reach this size.

There are three families of baleen whales: the right whales, the fin whales, and the gray whales. Blue whales are the largest species of fin whales. The chances are that you will never see one swimming about—but, actually, these whales are found in seas the world over. There is no particular area or ocean which they prefer.

These huge whales feed mainly on small fishes and on shrimplike creatures known as krill. The whale takes a huge mouthful of water and closes its mouth. Slowly it presses its tongue against the blades of baleen, which hang down from the upper jaw. In this way the seawater is strained off, and the food remains in the whale's mouth.

CAN BIRDS SMELL?

Living creatures tend to have, or develop, those senses which are necessary for them to survive. How important would the sense of smell be to a bird? Apparently, not very important, since the sense of smell seems to be almost or entirely missing in most birds.

What senses are important to birds? Well, a large part of the brain and nervous system of birds is connected with the senses of sight and balance—because they are important in flight. Fine eyesight is vital for a flying animal, and birds have remarkable eyesight.

They usually have a wide angle of vision. Many birds are also "out-eyed." Each eye looks out at right angles to the bird and sees a completely separate area.

The ability of birds to see color is more-or-less like that of a human. Night birds also have large lenses. This type of eye (in birds like owls) is able to gather and concentrate dim light.

The sense of hearing is excellent in birds. So are the senses of balance and of place in and movement through space. All these senses are centered in the ears. Many birds also have a good sense of taste. They can select their proper food instantly.

Most of the habits of birds are the inherited abilities we call instincts. Birds are born knowing almost everything needed to know to carry out their normal lives. They have no need to learn very much.

WHY DO WOODPECKERS PECK ON TREES?

Most of us, when we hear a woodpecker at work on a tree, imagine that it is harming the tree. The fact is, the opposite is true! The woodpecker is actually helping keep the tree alive.

First of all, the woodpecker is an arboreal bird; that is, it lives in trees. And it eats in trees. Hidden down deep in the crevices of the bark of trees are many grubs and insects. The woodpecker finds them with a kind of instinct—even when they cannot be seen on the outside. Then he drills a hole straight down to them and eats them. Quite often these insects and grubs are the kind that are harmful to the tree.

How can the woodpecker reach down into the wood? For one thing, the woodpecker's beak is sharp and strong and has a chisel-shaped point. Then the woodpecker also has an amazing tongue. In some species it is twice as long as the head itself.

The tongue is round and at the outer end has a hard tip with tiny barbs on the sides. Inside the beak the tongue is curled up like a spring. When the woodpecker goes after insects in the tree, it is able to thrust that tongue quite some distance from the beak and go far down into the crevices of the bark.

Woodpeckers don't always peck away at live trees. They use their chisel-like beak also for cutting holes in decayed wood. This is to make a place for their nests. They like trees which are hollow part of the way up.

Sometimes woodpeckers make two openings, like a front and back door. This is to enable them to get away if an unwelcome visitor should show up.

HOW DO SNAILS GET THEIR SHELLS?

Soft-bodied animals that have shells are known as mollusks. There are many different kinds of shell-bearing mollusks.

Some have two shells, or valves, which are hinged together. These mollusks are called bivalves. This group includes clams, oysters, scallops, and mussels. Other mollusks have only one shell, which may be cap-shaped but is usually twisted into a spiral. These mollusks are called snails.

The snail builds its shell like all mollusks. The shell is a mollusk's skeleton. The shell is part of the animal, and the mollusk is attached to it by muscles.

The soft animal inside can never leave its shell and return to it. As the mollusk grows bigger, its shell increases in size and strength. The shell is made of a form of limestone and is built by the mollusk itself. Of course, the mollusk does not know that it is building a home for itself.

In the case of the mollusk, certain glands are able to take limestone from the water and deposit it in tiny particles at the edge of, and along the inside of, the shell.

As a mollusk grows, its home becomes larger and stronger. Some of its shell glands contain coloring matter. As a result, a mollusk's shell may be spotted, all one color, or marked with lines.

Most mollusks live in the sea. None of the bivalves live out of water. Many snails, however, are air-breathing. These land snails are generally found in moist wooded places.

WHAT IS THE DIFFERENCE BETWEEN BACTERIA AND VIRUSES?

People usually link bacteria and viruses in terms of disease. But they are quite different from each other. Some bacteria cause disease, but most do not. There are at least two thousand species of bacteria, and most of them are either harmless or helpful.

A bacterium consists of only one cell. A single drop of sour milk may contain 100,000,000 bacteria. Bacteria are everywhere. Some live in the mouths, noses, and intestines of animals, including man. Others live on fallen leaves, dead trees, animal wastes, in fresh and salt water, in milk, and in most foods.

Since bacteria have some features of both plants and animals, scientists have not agreed on how to classify them. Most bacteria reproduce by fission—the cell divides in two.

Viruses are very small organisms, so small that they can only be seen in detail with an electron microscope. Viruses grow and multiply only when they are inside living cells. Outside living cells, viruses do not change in any way and seem lifeless. They cannot grow unless they are inside the cells of animals, plants, or bacteria.

Viruses that attack man and animals are called animal viruses. Those that attack plants are called plant viruses, and those that attack bacteria are called bacterial viruses.

The viruses that infect man and animals may be breathed in or swallowed, or enter through an opening in the skin. Some of them destroy cells simply by growing in them. Others cause the membranes separating two cells to dissolve, and still others cause cells to become malignant.

WHAT ARE LICE?

Sometimes when a person wants to describe something terrible he says, "It's lousy." "Lousy" is not a dirty word. It refers to the louse—which is a very obnoxious insect.

Actually, there are more than one thousand different insects that are called "louse" (plural: "lice"), but the one that people usually have in mind is the one that attacks human beings.

These are bloodsucking creatures. They are true parasites—their food is human blood. And these lice are more closely associated with man than any other members of the animal kingdom. This is because they exist upon his body during all stages of their development.

The "pediculus humanus" is typical of this kind of louse. It develops from eggs that are glued to the hair or clothing. In the hair, the eggs, or "nits" are sometimes easily seen. The body louse is passed from one person to another by wearing clothing from an infested person or by contact with bedding that is infested. The body louse is known to carry the disease typhus fever.

There is another kind of louse that attacks human beings and stays in hair in all parts of the body, including even the eyebrows. The control of these lice is done by dusting DDT powder or other insecticides under the clothing or in the hair.

An interesting thing about lice is that certain kinds attack other creatures as well. There are lice that live on birds, other mammals, and even lice that live on honey bees. There are also plant lice that suck the juices of plants.

WHY DO PEOPLE HUNT WALRUSES?

The walrus is a huge mammal that lives in Arctic waters off both coasts of northern North America and also off northeastern Siberia. It measures from eight to twelve feet in length when full-grown, and weighs up to three thousand pounds.

Walruses have a thick hide which is tough and wrinkled and which has almost no fur. Both the male and female walruses grow tusks which are used in digging for mollusks and for fighting.

Walruses live together in herds. They stay in far northern waters during the summer. In the fall they drift southward with the ice, and in the spring they swim northward again.

Walruses are hunted by man for many reasons. Eskimos and other Arctic peoples have depended on the walrus to supply them with food, fuel, clothing, and equipment. Practically every part of the body is used.

The blubber supplies oil for fuel. The leathery hides are used for clothing. The flesh is used for food. And the ivory tusks are used to make many different kinds of objects. Eskimos have used these tusks to carve small decorative objects that can be traded or sold.

WHAT IS THE 17-YEAR LOCUST?

There is no such thing! What is called the 17-year locust is really the 17-year cicada, an entirely different kind of insect. True locusts are grasshoppers, and calling the cicada a locust is a mistake that is commonly made.

The 17-year cicada is quite an unusual insect. It probably lives longer than any other insect (except perhaps the termite queen). Its life cycle goes like this:

the nymphs, the cicada's young, hatch from eggs on the twigs of trees. Then they drop to the ground.

Then they burrow into the ground and attach themselves to rootlets. And they remain there, without moving, as they suck the sap, for 17 years! Then instinct calls them out into the light.

Now they climb the trunk of a tree, and their skins split open. Out comes the mature cicada. For about five weeks they seem to live a happy life in the light of the sun. The males, and only the males, are able to make a piercing, metallic noise, the "voice" of the cicada. This sound is probably a mating call to the females.

The sound is made by one of the most complicated musical organs in nature. There are little drumlike plates at the base of the abdomen, and they are kept vibrating rapidly by muscles that seem never to get tired.

After the five weeks are over, the cicada dies. So it took 17 years to develop—for just five happy weeks of life. This 17-year cicada (in the South it matures in 13 years) is peculiar to the United States. Altogether, there are about one thousand species of cicada, and most of them live in the tropics.

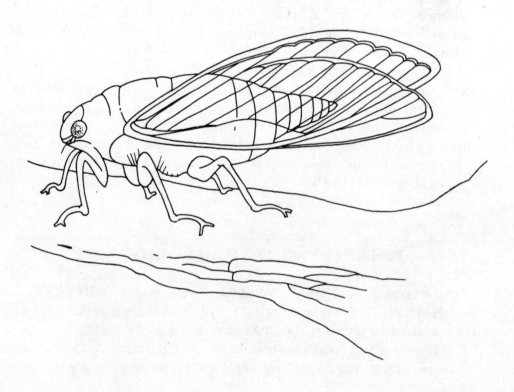

WHERE DO PENGUINS LAY THEIR EGGS?

During the Antarctic winter, February to October, the penguins live at sea. In October, which is early spring there, they come out of the sea and start a long trek to their rookeries, or breeding grounds.

The penguins may have to walk and slide, scramble and toboggan 60 miles across the sea ice to reach the rocky Antarctic coast. Usually the males arrive first and go directly to their nests of the previous year. The nests are made of stones. So you see, the penguins find a rocky area along the coast, where deep snow is not a problem, to lay their eggs.

The male and female penguin make a nest together before the eggs are laid. They go back and forth, collecting stones, carrying the stones in their beaks. They collect and guard the stones in turn. The stones are dropped by one partner; the other arranges them into a neat pile.

In mid-November the female penguin lays two bluish-white eggs. Now a very interesting process begins. The female and the male take turns guarding and hatching the eggs. After a certain period the female returns from the sea where she has been feeding and the male goes out to the sea to feed. Then he returns and she goes out to feed. But the timing is such that it is always the female who returns just as the chicks are coming out of their eggs. This taking turns in guarding and feeding goes on after the young are born for about four weeks.

WHY ARE DOLPHINS CONSIDERED INTELLIGENT?

Dolphins and porpoises are small whales, ranging in length from four to about twelve feet. Whether they are called "dolphins" or "porpoises" seems to be a matter of preference. Either name is correct.

There are several reasons why scientists consider the dolphin to be an unusually intelligent animal. Many of them have been known to imitate human speech quite distinctly—and without even being urged to do so. They can also learn to understand human words and respond to them.

Students of animal behavior have two other reasons for considering the dolphin intelligent. Dolphins are able to invent and play games. For example, suppose there is a feather floating about in a tank of water. A dolphin will get the feather and bring it near the jet of water entering the tank. The feather drifts into the jet and goes shooting off. The dolphin pursues it, catches it, brings it back, and again releases it into the jet.

Dolphins have invented games with small rubber inner tubes. They will toss the tube to someone standing by the tank and wait for the person to toss it back to them so they can catch it. This kind of play is considered a sign of intelligence.

Dolphins can also solve problems. If a piece of food is stuck under a rock, they can find a way to "blow" the food out from under the rock.

WHEN DID MAN FIRST FIND OUT ABOUT DINOSAURS?

No human being ever saw a living dinosaur. Dinosaurs were animals that lived in most regions of the world, but they died out everywhere about 65,000,000 years ago. It is believed that the first kind of man appeared less than 2,500,000 years ago. So dinosaurs were extinct by the time man appeared.

We know about dinosaurs from their remains. These are bones, found either in skeletons or separately; footprints in rock; impressions of skin, also in rock; and eggs.

There is some doubt as to when the first recognizable dinosaur bones were discovered. Footprints have been known for many years. A dinosaur skeleton may have been seen at Haddonfield, New Jersey, toward the end of the 1700's.

The first bones that are still available for examination and identification are some that were discovered in England. One set was found in 1822 and is now in the British Museum of Natural History in London.

Another set of dinosaur bones, found about the same time, was the basis for the first scientific description of any dinosaur. This was done in 1824 by a professor at Oxford University.

So you can see that man has found out about dinosaurs quite recently. Dinosaur specimens have been found in great numbers in the United States, Canada, Argentina, Brazil, India, Africa, Australia, Mongolia, China, France, Germany, Portugal, and the Soviet Union. This indicates that dinosaurs really lived all over the world.

WHAT IS AN AMOEBA?

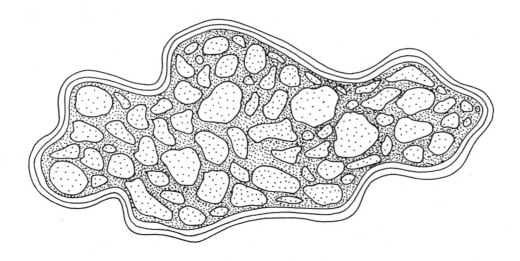

When we use the word "animal" we tend to think of pretty large creatures that move about on earth. But did you know that the amoeba is considered an "animal"?

It is a jellylike one-celled creature, so small that it can be seen only under a microscope. The common species of amoeba lives in freshwater streams and ponds, while other amoebas live on the bottom of fresh- and salt-water bodies, and in damp soils and foods.

The amoeba constantly changes its shape. It moves by pushing out one side and then another. As some of the jellylike substance is pushed out, it forms what are called false feet, or "pseudopodia." When the pseudopodia reach food, they wrap themselves around it and take it into the main body. This is the way the amoeba eats—it has no mouth.

The amoeba belongs to the Protozoa, which is the lowest division of the animal kingdom. It has no lungs or gills. But it absorbs oxygen from the water, gives off carbon dioxide, and digests its food, as more complex animals do.

The amoeba even seems to have feeling. If it is touched or disturbed, it immediately rolls itself into a tiny ball. The amoeba also tries to avoid bright light and water that is too hot or too cold.

In a full-sized amoeba, the nucleus, a tiny dot in the center of the protoplasm, divides into two parts. After this the amoeba itself divides, forming into new individual animals. When these become full-grown, each of them may divide again.

CHAPTER 6
LOVE, FAMILIES, AND BABIES

AT WHAT AGE DO PEOPLE FALL IN LOVE?

There is no specific age when this happens, but a person must be mature in certain ways to experience love. Young people do feel strong attachments for each other, and imagine at times they are "in love." But the full, deep meaning of loving another person can only be understood when one is mature. There is a responsibility that comes with love, and a dedication of oneself to the person one loves, that very young people cannot feel as yet.

IS A MOTHER'S LOVE FOR HER CHILDREN THE SAME AS HER LOVE FOR HER HUSBAND?

No. And it shouldn't be. It is not a question of "less love" or "more love," it is simply a different kind of love. A mother can love a child "with all her heart," and this will mean being devoted to the child, caring for it, helping it in every way, being close and warm and under-

standing, and even sacrificing for the child. But it is still different than the love for her husband.

That love — for her husband — involves her in a different way. It shows itself, among other things, in wanting to be physically close to him, in making love (having sexual intercourse). It reaches a beautiful closeness that is just as precious to her as closeness to her children — and it need not conflict with the love for her children.

IS IT POSSIBLE TO LOVE A FRIEND AS MUCH AS A SWEETHEART?

Of course. But it will be a different feeling with a dear friend. Having good times together, enjoying each other's company, admiring a friend, even feeling completely devoted to a friend, all this is a kind of "love." At the same time, one can feel strong emotional attachment to a sweetheart. Each has its place in our lives.

CAN PEOPLE OF DIFFERENT RACES FALL IN LOVE?

Yes, and often do. They have been doing it for thousands of years all over the world.

But society hasn't made it easy for such people. Laws have even been passed in certain places forbidding relationships or marriages between people of different races, in some cases because of prejudice, or ignorance about the other race, or a feeling that it is harmful to "mix" races.

Many people today feel it is perfectly natural and acceptable for men and women of different races to love each other and marry.

WHY DO PEOPLE SOMETIMES FALL OUT OF LOVE?

There is no single or simple explanation. It is sad when it happens, and seems to be something beyond "control." A person may simply begin to feel that he or she is no longer happy in the relationship. New interests or tastes by one of the partners can often bring it about. Sometimes people realize they didn't really love each other much in the first place, or were unsuited to each other.

AS MARRIED PEOPLE GET OLDER DO THEY LOVE EACH OTHER LESS?

If they loved each other all their lives together, then they still will when they are older. But the expression and quality of that love may change with age. Instead of passion, there may be tenderness. Instead of a desire to kiss, hug, and make love, there may be only the need and desire to be together, keep each other company, take care of each other. This stage of love can be just as meaningful and beautiful to older people as their young love was.

DO THE CHILDREN IN A FAMILY ALWAYS LOVE EACH OTHER?

Unfortunately, no. It often happens that there is jealousy, or basic differences in character, temperament or interests that set children in a family against each other. It has happened in many families for thousands of years.

But usually, even if they don't all "love" each other, the children in a family still feel the close ties and are concerned with each other.

CAN A CHILD HATE HIS FATHER OR MOTHER?

At any early age, many children say, "I hate you, Daddy!" or, "I hate you, Mommy!" And they feel they really do. This may be because of enforced discipline, or because of attitudes or opinions the parents have, or because certain things the children feel they want are being denied to them.

As these children grow older, they realize that they didn't really "hate" the father or mother, and may even forget they ever felt that way.

But there are cases where a child really does hate his parent or parents. There may be many reasons for this, but it is a sign that "something went wrong" in the relationship. Sometimes the parents are to blame. Their lack of understanding of the child, or the way they treated the child, may be responsible. In other cases, the child may be wrong in his own attitudes and feelings, bringing about "hate."

Whatever the reason, such things do happen and cause much unhappiness to children and parents.

WHY DO WE SOMETIMES FEEL THAT NOBODY LOVES US?

Because sometimes nobody does — at least, in the way we want to be loved. We all want other people, friends and parents, to think of us, remember us, do things for us. Sometimes these "other people" don't do it exactly when — and in the way — we'd like. They may have their own problems and disappointments, or be busy, or simply forget.

But very often those same people — our parents and friends — later *do* come through and show they love us. It's a mighty good feeling when that happens!

DOES A PARENT HAVE TO LIKE THE PERSON
WE FALL IN LOVE WITH?

We *hope* they do. We *wish* they did. Because that would give us a feeling of all being together, and of approval, and of the person we fell in love with being accepted.

But in some cases it doesn't happen. Some young people today are not even asking their parents' approval of the person they're going to marry.

So there is no "must" about it. It varies from family to family, depending upon the relationship. But it *is* nice when it happens.

IF WE "LOVE" A PET, LIKE A DOG OR A HORSE,
IS THAT REALLY LOVE?

It is a natural, wonderful, even exciting kind of love one can have for a pet — but it's not the same kind of love one can feel for another person. The great thing about it is that one can feel both kinds of love at the same time, enjoy them both, and still know which is really the more important and more meaningful.

ARE THERE SOME PEOPLE WHO NEVER FALL IN LOVE?

Yes. It doesn't mean they can't, or don't want to. It may be because they've never met the right person for them. Or it sometimes happens that certain people are "afraid" to fall in love, because it would mean changing their way of life, assuming responsibilities, sharing their home and possessions with someone else. Such people may love their parents, or brothers and sisters, but never be "in love."

WHAT DOES IT MEAN TO "LOVE YOUR FELLOW MAN"?

It means one should be concerned with other people, with their happiness, security, and progress. It means one should care what happens to other people, even if they are strangers, or quite different from ourselves. It means one should be willing to help them, even at some sacrifice to ourselves. Love for our fellow man is one of the basic principles of all great religions of the world.

DO ANIMALS FALL IN LOVE?

"Falling in love" among human beings involves not just sexual attraction, but also a mental and emotional involvement. Our whole person feels something for another individual's whole person.

But animals have a more limited attraction for each other. It is a sexual attraction that involves courtship and mating, but it takes place because of an instinct, the instinct to reproduce the species.

Sounds that are created, such as songs, colors that are displayed, such as in feathers of birds, certain "dances" that are done by animals and insects — all of these attract animals to each other. And this is quite different from what happens when humans fall in love.

WHAT DOES THE HEART HAVE TO DO WITH LOVE?

Nothing, really. The heart is like a pump in our body whose job it is to circulate our blood. And even though people will say, "I love you with all my heart," it is not in the heart that we feel all the things we do when we are in love. Still, the heart has become a kind of symbol of love.

Why did this happen? Probably because when we do feel a very strong emotion, the action of our heart is affected. When we're excited, the heart beats more rapidly. When we're frightened, our heart seems to "stand still." When we're upset or sad, our heartbeat slows up. So, since the heart reacts to what we are feeling, we have come to think of the heart as being the seat of love.

CAN PEOPLE WHO LOVE EACH OTHER LIVE TOGETHER WITHOUT GETTING MARRIED?

Of course they can, and many people have done it. Some young people today even feel that it's not "necessary" ever to get married formally.

There is no law that forces a man and woman who live together to be married — though members of certain religions are condemned by that religion if they don't.

But the society in which we live, including many of its laws and customs, is built around the idea of marriage. Wives have certain rights and protection that marriage gives them. Children of a legal marriage are entitled to certain things under law. And most people we meet believe in marriage and have strong attitudes about it.

So a couple that decides not to get married must be prepared to give up certain benefits, and face certain problems for themselves and their children. But they do have the right to make that choice.

WHY DO PEOPLE GO ON HONEYMOONS?

In very ancient times, a bridegroom had to "capture" his bride. He then would have to hide someplace with her until her relatives or tribespeople grew tired of searching for her. It is believed that the honeymoon developed as a symbol of what took place in those days.

So, to some extent, people still go on honeymoons because it is the traditional thing to do, just as they do many other "symbolic" things connected with marriage.

But newly married people enjoy going on a honeymoon because it gives them a chance to get to know each other intimately, and relate to each other. It is ideally spent in a place and atmosphere far from the bothers or problems of workaday life.

WHAT IS PUBERTY?

We say a young person has reached puberty when certain changes begin to take place in the body.

In a boy, hair (called "pubic hair") begins to grow in the genital area above the penis. Hair also starts to grow under the arms. The penis becomes larger. The voice becomes deeper. He begins to grow taller. All of these changes take place over a period of about two years.

In a girl, her breasts begin to develop. She also grows pubic hair. Her figure becomes larger and she may gain weight. Puberty can begin in a girl at the age of 11, but the average age is about 13 years.

WHAT IS ADOLESCENCE?

Adolescence is the period in a young person's life from puberty to adulthood. It begins in girls at ages from 11 to 15, and in boys about a year later. It lasts till they are about 19.

During the first period of adolescence, there is physical growth and change, and the sexual organs develop and begin to function.

During the last period of adolescence, many emotional changes take place, and problems may arise. The young person may feel adult in some ways, but still not want to act as an adult. New relationships with people will develop, and relationships with parents may be difficult. Adolescents begin to identify with groups of young people, or with some older person, or even form romantic attachments.

It is a period of so much change and development that the adolescent is constantly adjusting to new feelings in himself and in those he lives with.

WHY DOES IT USUALLY TAKE NINE MONTHS FOR A BABY TO BE BORN?

In mammals, the period between the fertilizing of an egg and the birth of the young that develops from that egg is called gestation. In human beings, the gestation period is about 280 days. It takes that long for all the changes and growth and development to take place so that the baby will be able to survive when it is born.

Among animals, the gestation period varies and is both longer and shorter than for human beings. For example: mice, 19 days; squirrels, 44 days; dogs, 63 days; horses, 336 days; elephants, 624 days.

IN WHAT PART OF A WOMAN'S BODY DOES THE BABY DEVELOP?

Almost immediately after the egg is fertilized, the cell begins to grow. It does this by cell division — one cell becomes two cells, and so on. It is now called an "embryo," and it still remains in the tube where fertilization took place, but it is moving toward the uterus, or womb.

Then it enters the uterus, and by the time the embryo is ten days old it begins to burrow its way into the walls of the uterus. Here is where it will grow and develop until it is ready to be born as a baby.

The uterus, a pear-shaped organ about the size of a fist, provides nourishment and protection for the developing child. As the baby grows, it stretches or expands. It can do this because the walls of the uterus are elastic, capable of being stretched to almost 500 times original size!

The baby is protected inside the uterus by two coverings. The outside covering keeps it attached to the wall of the uterus. The inside covering is filled with a liquid in which the baby floats. The liquid is like a cushion that protects the baby from being bumped while the mother moves about.

The baby grows and develops here until it is ready to be born.

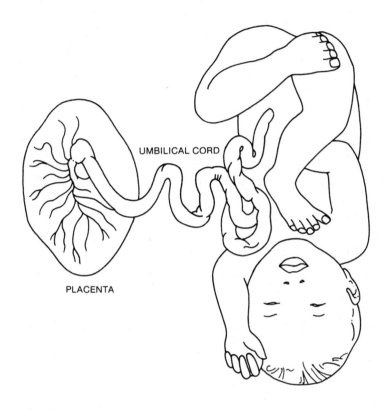

UMBILICAL CORD

PLACENTA

HOW DOES A BABY BREATHE INSIDE THE MOTHER'S BODY?

The baby receives oxygen — and nourishment — directly from the mother by means of a collection of blood vessels, called the "placenta," shaped like a flat cake. The placenta is connected to the embryo by a cord called the "umbilical cord."

Food, water, and oxygen from the mother's blood go into the blood vessels in this cord, and so into the baby. But the baby is already manufacturing its own blood, so the mother's blood doesn't go to the embryo.

WHAT EXACTLY HAPPENS IN THE PROCESS OF GIVING BIRTH TO A BABY?

The process is called "labor." It is the muscular contractions of the uterus which push the baby out into the world.

When the baby is ready to be born, the muscles of the uterus, or womb, start to contract. This is the first stage of labor. The muscles contract and relax, contract and relax. This may last from 9 to 14 hours.

WHEN DOES A BABY'S HEART BEGIN TO BEAT?

The heart of a baby is formed by joining of two blood vessels underneath the head. This tube grows quickly, bends around itself,

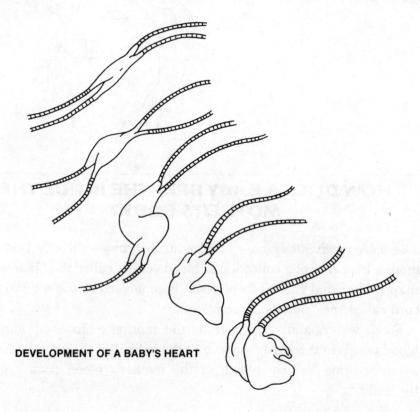

DEVELOPMENT OF A BABY'S HEART

and forms the structure that becomes the heart.

The heart begins to beat during the third week of the baby's life.

WHY ARE THERE SOMETIMES TWINS OR TRIPLETS INSTEAD OF ONE BABY?

Twins occur once in every 88 births. Triplets occur once in about 7,700 births.

There are two types of twins, fraternal and identical. Here is what happens to produce fraternal twins. A female has two ovaries where eggs are produced. It sometimes happens that one ovary releases two eggs at once, or each ovary releases an egg at the same time.

So there could be two eggs in one Fallopian tube, or an egg in each tube. Since these tubes are where sperm cells fertilize eggs, both eggs could become fertilized when sperm cells appear there.

If two eggs have been fertilized, each will become an embryo in the uterus, and will be born at the same time.

Fraternal twins may be of the same or opposite sex, and will only resemble each other as brothers and sisters do.

Identical twins are produced when a fertilized egg, after it is in the uterus, divides itself into two parts. Each part becomes an embryo, and both embryos develop and then are born at the same time.

Identical twins are of the same sex and look alike, which is why they are called "identical."

WHAT IS AN EMBRYO?

An embryo is a fertilized egg cell. It becomes an embryo the moment it is fertilized, because it begins to grow at once — from one cell to many cells.

"Embryo" is the term used for an unborn baby from the time of conception to the ninth or tenth week. At this time, vital organs are already formed and the unborn baby is called a "fetus."

DEVELOPMENT OF AN EMBRYO

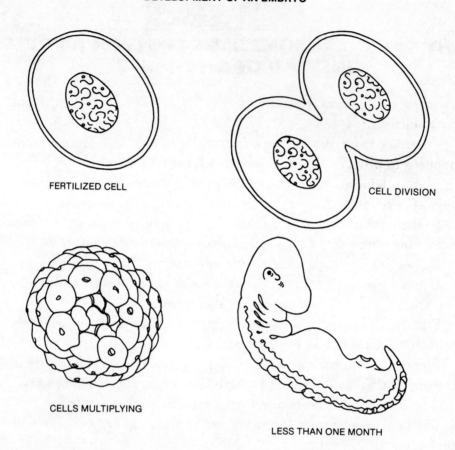

FERTILIZED CELL

CELL DIVISION

CELLS MULTIPLYING

LESS THAN ONE MONTH

WHAT IS A FETUS?

During the nine months the baby is in the mother's womb, it grows and develops.

At first it is called an embryo. An embryo is about an inch long at the end of six or seven weeks. In three months it is about four inches long.

At four months the embryo is six inches long, has arms and legs that can move, and is beginning to develop bones.

In general, however, the embryo is called a fetus after about the first two months of development.

IS IT TRUE THAT A HUMAN EMBRYO HAS A TAIL?

In the very first stages of life, embryos of all higher animals look so much alike that they cannot be told apart. Even in the third week of development, the embryo of a human being resembles that of a reptile, a bird, or another mammal.

So, during the first month, the human embryo does have a tail — which later disappears.

HOW BIG IS THE EMBRYO AT THE END OF ONE MONTH?

Here are the sizes of the embryo during its development. One month: about a quarter of an inch long. Two months: about one inch long.

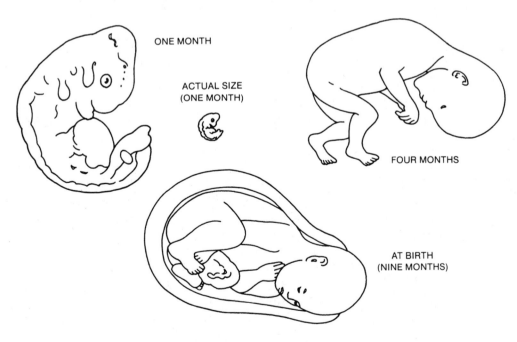

ONE MONTH

ACTUAL SIZE
(ONE MONTH)

FOUR MONTHS

AT BIRTH
(NINE MONTHS)

Three months: about four inches long. Four months: six inches long. It is usually termed a "fetus" after about the two-month period.

WHEN DOES THE FETUS BEGIN TO LOOK LIKE A HUMAN BABY?

It is hard to say exactly when this happens. But after eight weeks, when the embryo becomes a fetus, it definitely begins to look like an unborn human baby.

During the third month, the face changes a great deal. The eyes are in place, there is a bulging forehead, there are small, slit-like ears. There are nostrils, and a large, slit-like mouth. The upper limbs show the fingers, wrist, and forearms. By the end of the third month, the feet have toes, and the nails have begun to grow. There is no mistaking that it is a human baby now.

HOW DOES THE MOTHER KNOW WHEN THE BABY IS ABOUT TO BE BORN?

The baby will be born as the result of contractions of the uterus. The muscles of the uterus will squeeze tight, then relax, then squeeze tight, and so on. In this way it will push the baby out.

When these contractions begin, it is a sign that the baby is about to be born. The contractions feel like cramps, and are called "labor pains."

If the baby is actually on the way, the first few labor pains will be slight and about 15 to 30 minutes apart. Then, gradually, the pains become more intense, last longer, and happen more frequently.

When a woman feels this taking place, she knows the baby is about to be born and goes to the hospital.

In some cases, there is another sign: a small amount of water may pass out of the vagina, caused by the breaking of the water-filled sac in which the baby was lying during pregnancy.

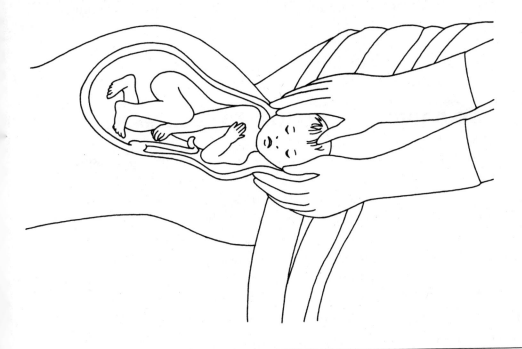

IS A BABY ALWAYS BORN HEAD FIRST?

Almost always. But sometimes the buttocks comes out first, in which case it is called a "breech" delivery. Or the face, or the shoulders, or the legs may come out first.

A doctor can often tell weeks ahead if something like this is going to happen. He then may be able to change the baby's position before it is born. He moves the baby around from outside the womb.

A baby that doesn't come out head first usually takes longer to be born.

WHY DO NEW BABIES CRY SO MUCH?

A new baby cries because it may be uncomfortable, or it may be hungry. As it gets older, it can hold more food in its stomach at each feeding — so it doesn't cry as often out of hunger.

Sometimes babies cry because it's like a form of exercise for them. They may not want or need anything — and still do a lot of crying.

DO BABIES LEARN HOW TO SUCK MILK?

Babies are born with a sucking instinct, and they have strong sucking muscles to help them do it, so they don't have to learn how to suck.

But nursing includes swallowing the milk the baby sucks in, and a baby has to learn how to swallow during its first few feedings.

At first the baby doesn't get milk from the breast, but a liquid called "colostrum." It is watery and yellowish, and contains food plus certain substances that help protect the baby from infections. Then, about three to five days after the birth of the baby, the mother's milk appears in her breasts.

WHY DO CHILDREN RESEMBLE THEIR PARENTS?

In a child, certain things from both parents are mixed together. The male sperm cell and the female egg cell contain chromosomes. A chromosome is made up of genes — and the genes are the particles that transmit hereditary characteristics. This means that those things about a father and mother that can be passed on to a child are passed on through the genes.

This includes such characteristics as color of skin, type of hair, shape of face, body structure, and many other things about the person.

The way the genes mix — and the type of genes that come from the father and mother — decide what the new baby will be like. It may have hair like the mother's, a nose like the father's, and some features that don't resemble either one.

WHAT COLOR WOULD A BABY BE IF ONE PARENT WAS BLACK AND ONE WAS WHITE?

If the black parent has no white ancestors, and the white parent has no black ancestors, their children would usually be an "in-between" color, and called "mulattoes."

If the two people are mulattoes, their children may vary in skin color from black (going back to the black ancestor) to white (the color of the white grandparent or ancestor).

If one parent is light in skin color, but has black ancestry, and marries a white, the children will usually have skin color no darker than that of the near-white person.

WHY ARE BABIES "BURPED" AFTER FEEDING?

"Burping" a baby means holding it erect over the adult's shoulder and patting it gently on the back. It is done after each feeding and sometimes during the feeding.

Burping gives the contents of the baby's stomach a chance to settle toward the bottom. It also gives the air, which was swallowed with the milk, a chance to come up and be expelled.

HOW OFTEN IS A NEWBORN BABY FED?

Newborn infants require food about once every four hours. If the baby is smaller, it may have to be fed once every three hours. It depends on how long it takes for the baby's stomach to become empty — and this doesn't always happen on an exact schedule. During its first month, a baby usually has to be fed six or seven times a day.

HOW MANY HOURS DOES A NEWBORN BABY SLEEP?

A newborn baby sleeps 18 to 20 hours a day. Each period of sleep lasts from two to three hours, and then the baby is awakened by hunger.

As the baby grows older, and its stomach becomes larger, it can hold more food, so it can sleep longer each time.

When a baby is six months old, it sleeps less, about 16 to 18 hours a day, and it usually can sleep through the night without being fed.

INDEX

A

Aardvarks, 132
Aaron, 20
Aborigines, 62
Abscesses, 75
Aconcagua, Mount, 57
Action Comics, 16
Adams, John, 28
Adhesives, 94–95
Adler, Charles, 24
Adolescence, 153–54
Adrenal glands, 72
Africa, 43, 57, 60, 62, 124, 142
Air, 38, 46, 65, 71, 103
Alaska, 51, 98
Albert, Prince, 27
Alcoholic beverages, 37, 77
Aleutian Islands, 51
Alexandria, 30
Algae, 40, 132
Alimentary canal, 74
Alligators, 97
Alpaca, 102
Alpha Centauri, 95
Alphabets, 15
Altes Museum (Berlin), 30
Amber, 35
Amendments, Constitutional, 37
American Revolution, 27–29
Amoebas, 143
Amphibians, 131, 132

Anderson, Elbert, 29
Angles, 14
Anglican Church, 106
Annelids, 119
Antarctica, 59, 141
Anteaters, 132
Apes, 126
April Fools' Day, 18–19
Arabia, 7, 25, 26, 29, 31
Argentina, 57, 142
Armadillos, 132
Arteries, 79
Asia, 22, 58, 91, 124
Astronomy, 95, 103
Athena, 56
Athens, 10, 56
Athletics, 33–34
Atmosphere, 46, 57–58, 65
Atoms, 64, 109–10
Australia, 57, 62, 96, 117, 142
Autopsy, 92–93
Aztecs, 106

B

Babies, 76, 154–164
Babylon, 7, 15, 22
Bacteria, 83–84, 100, 137–38
Bakers, 13
Baleen, 134

Balkan Peninsula, 31
Bantu, 62
Barbers, 10–11
Basal ganglia, 69
Bats, 126
Bears, 16, 131
Bees, 118–19, 139
Bible, 20, 63, 99–100
Bicycles, 105–6
Bill of Rights, 37
Birds, 117–18, 123–24, 131, 135–36,
    139
Birth, 156, 160, 161
Bivalves, 136, 137
Blood, 72–73, 79
Blue whales, 134–35
Boas, 114, 115
Bobbies, 11–12
Bohr, Niels, 64
Bonds, 53, 54
Borglum, Gutzon, 41
Borglum, Lincoln, 41
Boston, 9
Boxing, 33, 34
Brain, 69–70, 77, 132
Bran, 23
Brazil, 132, 142
Bread, 12–13
Breast-feeding, 162
Breathing, 71
Breech delivery, 161
Bricks, 109
British Museum, 30
British Museum of Natural
    History, 142
Brooches, 35
Brown rice, 23
Burping, 163
Bushmen, 62
Butter, 99–100
Butterflies, 128–29
Byerly Turk, 7

C

Cacti, 49–50
Calcium, 22, 38
California, 51, 96
Camels, 22
Cameos, 35
Canada, 97, 108, 142
Cancer, 68
Canines, 16
    See also Dogs
Cannibals, 60
Capillaries, 79
Capitol, 28
Carbon, 38, 71, 86, 102, 108, 110
Carbon dioxide, 36, 59, 72, 73, 143
Carbon-14 dating, 91–92
Carbonic acid, 76
Caribou, 22
Casein, 22
Cashmere, 102
Caspian Sea, 55
Cathedral of St. John the Divine, 41
Cats, 125, 129–31
Cement, 85–86
Central America, 50, 51, 132
Central Standard Time, 21
Centrifugal force, 106
Cerebellum, 69, 70
Cerebral palsy, 69
Cerebrum, 70
Chariot races, 7, 34
Charles IX, King of England, 18
Checkers, 29–30
Cheese, 84, 100
Chemical elements, 63, 71
Chess, 29
Chicago American, 15
Children, 144–45, 147–48, 151–52, 162,
    163
Chile, 51, 57
China, 15, 22–23, 51, 57, 106, 142
Chlorophyll, 49

Christmas trees, 27
Chromosomes, 162
Cicadas, 139–40
Citizens, rights of, 37
Clams, 136
Clay, 109
Climate, 43, 59, 65
Coal, 43
Cod, 121
Colonial America, 58, 63
Color blindness, 125–26
Colors, 88
Colostrum, 162
Columbus, Christopher, 28, 61
Comic books, 15–16
Concrete, 85
Condors, 123
Conger eels, 112
Congo, 60
Congress, U.S., 28, 29, 37
Conifers, 40
Connecticut, 63
Conquistadores, 125
Constitution, U.S., 37
Continental drift, 43
Cook, Captain James, 13
Copper, 63, 99
"Cops," 12
Coral, 35
Coronado, Francisco, 125
Cortes, Hernando, 125
Cotyledons, 38–39
Cows, 22, 96, 131
Coyotes, 16
Crete, 34
Crocodiles, 133
Crying, 161–62

D

Dalton, John, 64
Dams, 91, 107–8
Dance, 33

Darley Arabian, 7
Deficiency diseases, 79–80
Demersal eggs, 121
Denmark, 27, 60
De Soto, Hernando, 125
Detergent, 87
Diamonds, 20, 86–87
Diatoms, 39–40
Dinosaurs, 40, 133–35, 142
Dionysus, 10
Discus throwing, 34
Dissonance, 90
Dogs, 16–17, 125, 131, 149, 154
Dolphins, 141–42
Draughts, 29
Druids, 27
Dutch, 14

E

Eagles, 123, 132
Earache, 66
Earrings, 25–26, 35
Earthquakes, 51
Earthworms, 38, 119–20
Eastern Standard Time, 21
Echo sounders, 100–101
Ecology, 54
Eels, 112–13
Eggs, 112, 120–22, 131, 132, 141
Egypt, 7, 10, 13, 15, 17, 20, 23, 25–27,
    29, 30, 33–35, 42, 60, 94, 106, 108
Elbrus, Mount, 57
Elephants, 131, 154
Elevators, 8–9
Embankment dams, 107–8
Embryos, 38–39, 154, 157–60
Emeralds, 20, 35
Emus, 117
Endocrinology, 71–72
England, 7, 9, 11, 27, 29, 60, 94, 142
English language, 14, 15, 34
Epidermis, 80

Epiglottis, 73, 74
Ericson, Leif, 61
Eskimos, 22, 97–98, 139
Esophagus, 73–74
Etruscans, 35
Europe, 22, 31, 57, 58, 124
Everest, Mount, 57
Evolution, 43
Eyes, 114, 122, 123, 129, 130, 135

F

Falcons, 123
Fathers, 148
Fermentation, 84
Ferns, 40
Fetus, 157–60
Fibers, 109–10
Fiji, 60
Fire, 36
Fire departments, 9
Fish, 40, 112, 120–23, 131
Fisher, Bud, 15
Flowering plants, 41, 50
Flying chair, 8
Folk songs, 59–60
Foxes, 16
France, 18, 23, 30, 60, 142
Frankincense, 106
Franklin, Benjamin, 9
Fraternal twins, 157
French Revolution, 30
Friends, 146, 148
Fungi, 49

G

Gasoline, 102–3
"General Stud Book," 7
Genes, 162
Geology, 43
Germany, 27, 30, 108, 142

Gestation, 154
Glaciers, 55, 58–59
Glands, 72
Glue, 94–95
Goats, 96–97, 102
Godolphin Arabian, 7
Godwin Austin, Mount, 57
Gold, 34–35, 63, 99
Golf balls, 93–94
Gout, 77–78
Grapes, 96
Gravity dams, 107
Great Lakes, 55–56
Greece, 7, 8, 10, 13, 18, 25, 29, 30, 33,
    35, 51, 56, 64, 96
Greek language, 14, 15, 54
Greenland, 59–61, 97
Greenwich, England, 21, 24
Guido d'Arezzo, 32
Gyroscopic force, 105–6

H

Hair, 80–81
Halibut, 121
Harmony, 90
Haugh, Harry, 24
Hawaii, 13, 57
Hawks, 123
Hearing, 130, 135
Heart, 76–77, 151, 156–57
Heat, 36, 78
Hebrews, 25, 106
Helicopters, 98
Hematite, 108
Hemoglobin, 72–73
Hereditary characteristics, 162
Herring, 121
Hessians, 27
Hibernation, 127
Hieroglyphics, 15
Hindus, 100, 106

Hippopotamus, 130–31
Histidin, 82
Homer, 7, 29
Honeymoons, 152–53
Hormones, 71–72
Hornets, 118
Horses, 7, 22, 94, 96, 97, 124–26, 131,
    149, 154
Humus, 38
Husbands, 144–45
Hydraulic cement, 86
Hydraulic power, 9
Hydrogen, 38, 71, 102, 110
Hyenas, 113–14

I

Ice Age, 51, 55, 58–60
Iceland, 60
Identical twins, 157
Ideographs, 15
Igloos, 97–98
Incas, 106
Incense, 106
Income tax, 37, 52
India, 14, 22, 23, 25, 31, 51, 142
Indians, 58, 125
Indonesia, 51
Indoor plumbing, 34
Inflation, 52
Ingstad, Helge, 61
Inhibitions, 77
Insects, 118–19, 128–29, 131, 132, 136,
    138–39
Instincts, 135, 162
International Date Line, 21
Ionosphere, 57
Iran, 51
Ireland, 60
Iron, 38, 73, 108
Irrigation, 90–91, 107
Italy, 31, 35, 45, 60

J

Jackals, 16
Jaguars, 132
Japan, 23, 51
Jasper, 35
Jaundice, 67
Javelin throwing, 34
Jefferson, Thomas, 41
Jellyfish, 121–22
Jewelry, 25–26, 34–35
Jews, 25, 106
Jockey Club, 7
Jokes, 18
Jupiter, 47
Jutes, 14

K

Kamchatka, 51
Kangaroos, 97
Kant, Immanuel, 76
Kashmir, 57
Keys, 17–18
Khafre, King, 42
Kilimanjaro, Mount, 57
Knots, 24–25
Krill, 135
Kosciusko, Mount, 57
K2, 57
Kurile Islands, 51

L

Labor, 156, 160
Lactose, 22
Lapland, 22
Larynx, 73, 74
Laser beams, 105
Lava, 44–45
Latin, 14, 15, 62, 127, 131

Latin America, 14
See also Central America; South
   America
Latitude, 24
Laughing hyenas, 113–14
Lead, 103
Leather, 96–97
Leavening, 12–13
L'Enfant, Major Pierre, 28
Leopards, 129
Leukocytes, 75
Lice, 138–39
Light, 88–89, 105
Light-years, 95
Lincoln, Abraham, 41
Lions, 129
Lizards, 97
Llamas, 102
Locks, 17–18
London, 9, 11–12, 35
Longitude, 24
Louvre, 30
Love, 144–52
Lungs, 71, 72, 131, 132, 134
Lymph nodes, 75

M

McKinley, Mount, 57
Mackerel, 121
Magma, 43–44
Magnesium, 38
Magnetite, 108
Mammals, 131–32, 139
Marriage, 146, 147, 151–52
Mars, 47
Marsupials, 127
Maryland, 28
Massachusetts, 58, 63

Mauna Kea, 57
Measurements, 23–24
Medes, 25
Medicine, 105
Medulla, 69
Melanin, 81, 82
Melody, 90
Mercury, 47
Metals, 63
Metric system, 23–24
Mexico, 51, 125
Miacis, 16
Mice, 131, 154
Micro-organisms, 38
Middle Ages, 31, 35
Milk, 22
Minerals, 23, 63
Mistletoe, 27
Mohair, 102
Mollusks, 136–37
Money, 51–53
Mongolia, 142
Monkeys, 126
Moon, 45–46
Moors, 29
Moray eels, 112, 113
Mortar, 85
Mosquitoes, 67–68
Mothers, 144–45, 148
Motor cortex, 69
Mountain Standard Time, 21
Mountains, 57–58
Mulattoes, 163
Mummies, 26–27
Muses, 30
Museums, 30
Mushrooms, 48–49
Music, 90
Musical notes, 32
Mussels, 136
"Mutt and Jeff," 15
Mysticeti, 134

N

Nautical miles, 25
Nepal, 57
Neptune, 47
Nero, 48
Neumes, 32
New Fun, 16
New Guinea, 51, 60
New Year's Day, 18–19
New York City, 9, 11–12, 41
New York *Gazette and General
        Advertiser,* 29
New Zealand, 60
Newfoundland, 61
Niacin, 80
Nicaragua, 132
Nicotine, 74
Nile River, 90
Nitrogen, 38, 71, 84
North America, 57, 60–61, 123–25, 139
Norway, 27, 60, 108
Notation, 32

O

Ocean depths, 100–101
Octane, 103
Odontoceti, 134
Olive oil, 56
Olympic games, 33–34, 56
Opossums, 127–28
Orbits, 45, 47
Orchestras, 30
Ores, 63
Ostriches, 117–18
Otis, Elisha, 9
Ovaries, 72
Owls, 135
Oxford University, 142
Oxygen, 36, 38, 39, 65, 69, 71–73, 102,
        110, 143, 155

Oysters, 136
Ozone, 65

P

Pacific Standard Time, 21
Padlocks, 18
Panama Canal, 67
Pancreas, 72
Papillae, 78
Parallax, 95
Parathyroids, 72
Parents, 148, 149, 162, 163
Parma, Italy, 10
Pearls, 35
Peel, Sir Robert, 11
Pelagic eggs, 121
Pellagra, 80
Penguins, 141
Persia, 7, 23, 25, 106
Petroleum, 49
Pets, 149–50
        See also Cats; Dogs
Phagocytes, 75
Philadelphia, 9
Philippines, 51
Phoenicia, 13
Phonetics, 15
Phonograms, 15
Phosphorus, 22, 38
Photoelectric cell, 88–89
Pierced ears, 25–26
Pigs, 96, 97, 130, 131
Pines, 40
Pit vipers, 114–16
Pituitary, 72
Placenta, 155
Planets, 47
Plants, 37–41, 43, 49, 71, 138, 139
Platinum, 63
Plato, 29
Play-party songs, 59–60
Plumbing, 34

Polar bears, 127
Police, 11–12
Polymerization, 110
Polynesia, 60
Polyps, 121–22
Pompeii, 45
Porphyry, 44
Porpoises, 141–42
Portugal, 142
Potassium, 38
Potomac River, 28
Practical jokes, 18
President, U.S., 37
Protein, 22
Protozoa, 143
Puberty, 153
Pulse rate, 76–77
Purines, 78
Pus, 75

R

Rabbits, 131
Raccoons, 16
Racially mixed relationships, 146, 163
Radar, 110, 126
Radiocarbon dating, 91
Railroads, 20
Raisins, 96
Rattlesnakes, 115–16
Rebec, 31
Reed, Walter, 67
Reindeer, 22
Religion, 10, 33, 60, 63, 100, 106, 150, 151
Reptiles, 131–33
Reservoirs, 91, 107, 108
Resins, 106
Rheas, 117
Riboflavin, 80
Rice, 22–23, 91
Rings, 35
Roman Catholic Church, 32, 63, 106

Romans, 10, 13, 18, 25, 27, 29, 34, 35, 56, 62, 86, 106
  See also Latin
Roosevelt, Theodore, 41
Rubies, 20
Rushmore, Mount, 41
Russia, 60, 108
  See also Soviet Union
Rutherford, Ernest, 64

S

St. Paul's Cathedral, 9
Salmon, 120
Saluting, 32–33
Sapphires, 20
Satellites, 103–4
Saturn, 47
Saxons, 14, 27
Scallops, 136
Scalping, 58
Scandinavia, 14
Scarabs, 20
Scotland Yard, 11
Scurvy, 80
Sedimentary rocks, 49
Seeds, 38–41
Senators, 37
17-year locusts, 139–40
Sewers, 34
Sexual intercourse, 145
Sheep, 22, 102
Sheridan, General Philip, 41
Ships, 24–25
Sholes, Christopher, 19
Siberia, 139
Sight, *see* Eyes
Siemens, Werner von, 9
Silver, 35, 63, 98–99
Slavery, 37
Sleep, 75–76
Sloths, 132
Smell, sense of, 79, 120, 128–30, 135

Smoking, 74
Snails, 136–37
Snakes, 97, 114–16
Soap, 87
Social insects, 118
Soil, 37–38, 119–20
Soldiers, 32–33
Sonar, 110–11
South America, 43, 50, 51, 57, 60, 116,
    117, 123, 124, 132
Soviet Union, 57, 142
    See also Russia
Spain, 14, 29, 31, 60, 96
Spallanzani, Lazzaro, 126
Speed measurement, 24–25
Sphinx, 42–43
Spillways, 108
Spirituals, 60
Sports, 33
Squirrels, 154
Stars, 95
Steam power, 9
Steel, 108
Stocks, 53–54
Stradivari, Antonio, 31
Stratosphere, 57
Sturges, Joshua, 29
Sucking instinct, 162
Sulfur, 38, 99
Sun, 45–48, 65, 88, 95
Sunburn, 81–82
Sunsets, 47–48
Superior, Lake, 55, 108
Superman Quarterly Magazine, 16
Surfactants, 87
Surfing, 13–14
Surgery, 11
Swallowing, 73–74
Sweden, 27, 60, 108
Sweethearts, 146
Swiss cheese, 100
Swords, 33

Synthetic fibers, 109–10
Syria, 7

T

Tanning, 97
Taste, sense of, 78–79, 128–29, 135
Taxation, 37, 51–52
Teatro Farnese, 10
Technology, 30
Telescopes, 95
Testes, 72
Theaters, 10
Thiamin, 80
Thoroughbred horses, 7
Thymus, 72
Thyroid, 72
Tigers, 129, 130
Time zones, 20–21
Toadstools, 48–49
Tomarctus, 16
Tompkins, Daniel D., 29
Tongue, 78
Traffic signals, 24
Trees, 40, 136
Triplets, 157
Troposphere, 57–58, 65
Turkey, 7, 51
Turquoise, 35
Turtles, 134
Twins, 157
Typewriter keys, 19
Typhus fever, 138
Tyrosin, 82

U

Ultrasonic sounds, 126
Ultraviolet light, 65, 81, 82
Umbilical cord, 155
"Uncle Sam," 28–29
Universal keyboard, 19
Uranus, 47

Uric acid, 78
Uterus, 154, 160

V

Venus, 47
Vertebrates, 131
Vesuvius, Mount, 45
Victoria, Queen, 27
Vicuna, 102
Vielle, 31
Vikings, 14, 60–61
Vinland, 61
Violins, 30–31
Vipers, 114–16
Virgin wool, 102
Virginia, 28
Viruses, 67, 68, 83, 137–38
Vision, *see* Eyes
Vitamins, 23, 40, 79–82, 84
Volcanoes, 44–45
Volunteer fire companies, 9
Voting rights, 37
Vultures, 123–24

W

Walruses, 139
Wander cells, 75
War of 1812, 29
Warts, 83
Washington, George, 28, 41
Washington, D.C., 20, 28, 41
Wasps, 118
Water, 34, 36, 38, 50, 65, 90, 91
Water buffalo, 22
Wegener, Alfred, 43
West Indies, 60
Whales, 40, 134–35
Whiskers, 130
White rice, 23
Wilson, "Uncle Sam," 28–29

Windpipe, 74
Windsor Castle, 27
Wine, 23
Witchcraft, 62–63
Wolves, 16
Woodpeckers, 136
Wool, 102
Words, 14
Worms, 119–20
Wrestling, 33, 34
Writing, 15

Y

Yaks, 22
Yale University, 24
Yeast, 12–13
Yellow fever, 67–68
Yellow jackets, 118